Peace or Pain

Discovering the unbroken you
and changing your relationship with pain

Peace or Pain -
Discovering the unbroken you and changing your relationship with pain

Cover design by Sally Page

Visit www.boundless-meditation.co.uk

To Stephen, Jasmine and Brodie.
You are all simply amazing.
Thank you for being part of my life.

To my teacher MKI and all Ishayas past and present,
I would not be who I am today without your guiding light.
Thank you from the bottom of my heart.

Contents

Acknowledgements

Introduction

Part One - My journey from pain to peace

Chapter 1   Desperation

Chapter 2   Searching for a solution

Chapter 3   Coming home

Chapter 4   Leap of faith

Chapter 5   Peace or pain

Chapter 6   Finding myself

Chapter 7   A brave new world

Chapter 8   Making the best of things

Part Two - Understanding pain

Chapter 9   The choice between peace and pain

Chapter 10   What is pain?

Chapter 11   The mind-body connection

Chapter 12   Mental, emotional, physical

Chapter 13   Fight or flight

Chapter 14   What is stress?

Chapter 15   Habitual patterns

Chapter 16   Self-preservation

Chapter 17   Awareness

Chapter 18   Content / Context

Chapter 19   The original blueprint

Part Three - Changing your relationship with pain

Chapter 20   Meditation demystified

Chapter 21   Ascension techniques

Chapter 22   Innocence and gentleness

Chapter 23   Commitment

Chapter 24   Surrender

Chapter 25   Ending the need to do something

Chapter 26   Emotional awareness / connection

Chapter 27   Find peace in the pain

Chapter 28   Prioritise your peace

Chapter 29   Pay attention

Chapter 30   Giving up the why

Chapter 31   Resistance is futile

Chapter 32   Accepting help

Chapter 33   You are already that which you seek

Chapter 34   Equal importance

Part Four - How to make the choice

Chapter 35   The right attitude

Chapter 36   Feel the body

Chapter 37   Loosen up

Chapter 38   Body rhythm

Chapter 39   Alert listening

Chapter 40   Surrender to the flow

Chapter 41   Into space

Chapter 42   Appreciation and gratitude

Chapter 43   Let your body be your guide

Chapter 44   Breath meditation

Chapter 45   Sound and vibration

Chapter 46   Moving your awareness

Chapter 47   Loving the skin you're in

Chapter 48   Keep making the choice

Appendix   Resources

               Suicide watch

Acknowledgments

So many people have been an inspiration in the writing of this book, but I must begin with my family.

Stephen, my husband who has been there for me through thick and thin, is my unwavering partner through life. I could not have even begun to write this book without his love and support. His love has always been freely given and unconditional, for that I am truly grateful.

Jasmine and Brodie, who have been there for me in more ways than they know, are the ongoing source of inspiration in my life. Without their unique flavours, kindness, and acceptance of my quirky and often unusual ways, I would not be the person I am today. I am in awe of all they have transcended in the journey through life so far. Their courage and tenacity are awe-inspiring. They spur me on to go for more every day!

My Mum has also been one of the biggest influences in my life. She is one of the kindest and most generous ladies I know, and I am blessed to know a lot of kind and generous people! My Mum has always been there for me in so many ways. She has spent many an hour searching for solutions to my health conditions and pain levels, always coming up with a variety of creative and useful solutions. And still, she has no idea how amazing she is. I hope when she reads these words, she will have an inkling of how important she is to me!

My closest friend and confidante Amanda is an amazing, kind, loving and very funny lady! Her sense of humour has kept me sane through good times and bad. She has been my biggest cheerleader through life and a great source of encouragement in writing this book.

Shukri Devi has been a huge help in all the support she has provided in the form of proofreading, editing and general encouragement in creating this book. She is always there for me in so many ways. My confidence has grown in the time we have been working together more closely and, for that, I am immensely grateful.

I am also grateful to Maitreya who provided guidance in publishing this book and who was so willing to help and support me with all the information I needed.

Maharishi Krishnananda Ishaya (MKI), who is my spiritual Teacher, has shown me what it is like to be seen and heard, so completely I am left dumbfounded. MKI has been a guiding light, he inspires me to go for gold and then keep going. His love and acceptance of me has been the foundation for my ability to step through all the distressing situations which have presented since he became my Teacher.

I must also thank all Ishayas who are a massive source of inspiration and encouragement in all I endeavour to do in this lifetime. I felt lost and bewildered, like a fish out of water, before I found the Ishayas of The Bright Path. When I learnt Ascension and was welcomed into the fold, I knew I was home, I had found my tribe. A community which provides total acceptance and love for whoever wishes to join is such food for the soul. Within this community I have been able to grow and find myself, becoming comfortable in my own skin at last. Thank you for always being there for me. I promise I will pay it forward forever.

Finally, my gratitude goes to all Ascenders and to you, the reader, for being willing to open up to new possibilities.

Introduction

This book is a way of sharing my own experience and discoveries with the world. Most of humanity is not aware of the choice they have in each and every moment. My hope is the following pages will help people to understand the choice they have and how to make it.

Pain, especially long-term chronic pain, is a tricky thing to manage. It is, however, absolutely possible to change your relationship with pain and transcend suffering altogether. This includes mental torment and emotional pain, as well as physical pain.

Pain is a natural function and a useful one to keep our body safe and functional. Pain is always possible; however, suffering is optional. Suffering, in a way, is like experiencing the pain twice.

There is a piece of text called 'Sallatha Sutta: The Arrow'* that describes the distinction between the initial pain and the secondary suffering that arises from our response to that initial pain.

Here is an extract from the Sutta:

. . .

"When touched with a feeling of pain, the uninstructed run-of the-mill person sorrows, grieves, & laments, beats his breast, becomes distraught. So he feels two pains, physical & mental. Just as if they were to shoot a man with an arrow and, right afterward, were to shoot him with another one, so that he would feel the pains of two arrows....

* Sallatha Sutta: The Arrow - translated from the Pali by Thanissaro Bhikkhu

.... As he is touched by that painful feeling, he is resistant. Any resistance-obsession with regard to that painful feeling obsesses him. Touched by that painful feeling, he delights in sensual pleasure. Why is that? Because the uninstructed run-of-the-mill person does not discern any escape from painful feeling aside from sensual pleasure.

.... Now, the well-instructed disciple of the noble ones, when touched with a feeling of pain, does not sorrow, grieve, or lament, does not beat his breast or become distraught. So he feels one pain: physical, but not mental.

.... No resistance-obsession with regard to that painful feeling obsesses him....

.... Sensing a feeling of pain, he senses it disjoined from it.... He is disjoined, I tell you, from suffering & stress....

.... This is the difference, this the distinction, this the distinguishing factor between the well-instructed disciple of the noble ones and the uninstructed run-of-the-mill person."

. . .

Although the Sutta talks about the first kind of pain as being physical, the same principle applies to emotional pain. Emotional pain is felt in the body, so when our feelings are hurt, this is also experienced physically. We often respond to hurt feelings by blaming the other person, or ourselves, and this results in a secondary pain we call suffering.

If you want to understand more about pain and the reaction of suffering, you will need to explore the mechanism that is in play from your own direct experience.

This book will break down the mechanism of pain in easy to understand parts. I will explain all the functions in play, and the approach we can use to change our relationship with pain, to prevent the secondary reaction of suffering from occurring.

I have laid out the information into four parts:

Part One - My journey from pain to peace

Part Two - Understanding pain

Part Three - Changing your relationship with pain

Part Four - How to make the choice

Part One is an outline of my personal experience, subsequent exploration and discoveries. Be warned, I reached rock-bottom and had nowhere left to turn, so the beginning is not pretty and could be disturbing for some.

Part Two covers everything you need to know so you can become more familiar with the internal process of pain and what could be complicating your experience.

Part Three discusses a variety of ways to begin gaining a clearer understanding of the unconscious mechanism of pain and suffering. It includes helpful suggestions on how to make a difference within your own experience of pain.

Part Four provides several exercises and further information on how to actually make the choice. You will also learn how to begin cultivating a sustainable experience of peace.

It's worth mentioning that I am not a medical doctor and cannot dispense advice on how to heal your body. All the information included in this book is based on my own individual experience and meant to inspire you to begin your own exploration.

It is important that you get any symptoms checked out by a qualified medical professional and do not rely solely on anything I suggest.

This book is more about changing your relationship with (and experience of) pain than it is about healing yourself. Healing is usually the natural by-product of exploring your relationship with pain, but nothing is guaranteed.

As I said before, pain is tricky. It takes determination and commitment to make a difference, to discover how to make the choice (and keep making the choice) until it becomes sustainable.

I know it is possible, because I have experienced it for myself. However, along the way there have been many pitfalls and setbacks. It has taken a great deal of tenacity to keep going. The journey continues for me as well. My curiosity will lead me to keep exploring to discover what else is possible!

Curiosity is what keeps my excitement and passion alive, ready for more discoveries and realisations. There is always more!

Stay open, don't believe a word I say so you always make it about your own experience. I can share what I have learnt, but at the end of the day, I can only open the door. The rest is up to you.

I will, of course, continue to share what I learn, and I will support people in their own exploration. Be sure to check out the resources section at the back of the book, if you are ready to begin (or continue) your own journey from pain to peace.

Part One
My journey from pain to peace

"How does one become a butterfly?"
She asked pensively.

"You must want to fly so much that you are
willing to give up being a caterpillar."

- Trina Paulus -

Chapter 1
Desperation

How did I get here?

'Here' is on my kitchen floor, sitting down in a crumpled heap. I'm holding a knife in my hand and I'm thinking of cutting my wrist and ending it all. I wasn't really thinking about dying. I just wanted the pain to stop. I was silently screaming inside myself.

Why does this hurt so much? Why won't the pain stop? I need it to stop. I can't take any more.

Nobody realised how much it hurt. Nobody could make it stop. Nobody.

. . .

My husband was crouched down beside me, a terrified look in his eyes. I knew he loved me, and I knew he would do anything for me. But what good is that when nothing can be done.

He was talking softly to me, trying to get me to put the knife down. I could tell he was scared to say the wrong thing, or get too close in case it made me use the knife. I was sorry to put him through this, but I was so desperate. I literally could take no more pain at that moment.

I was vaguely aware that he was holding our son in his arms, but I hadn't looked away from the knife since I had collapsed on the floor. It had taken a great deal of effort to get here, because I was unable to walk without assistance. I couldn't lift my right leg at all and could only get my left leg an inch off the floor, so I had dragged myself on crutches just to get here.

My condition is called Symphysis Pubis Dysfunction (SPD). It is a fairly rare condition, which started in the pregnancy of our second child. The child my husband was holding right now. I just had an ache in my hip to start with, which I told my midwife about. I was told not to complain, that I'd had a child before and should know you get aches and pains as part of the process. Except I hadn't experienced any aches or pains in my first pregnancy.

My first pregnancy was easy. This was new, but I felt that I was making a fuss, so I kept quiet and carried on in silence. The ache got a bit worse and a few other places started to hurt too, but it wasn't too bad, so I stayed quiet.

It wasn't until I was about 32 weeks pregnant that my legs collapsed from underneath me and I fell over. Then I was told, I should have said something earlier. That was rather infuriating obviously, because I had said something. I was given little to no help because there was apparently nothing that could be done. I have since learnt that this is not entirely true.

I had a pair of crutches left over from a sprained ankle. They were mismatched and very old, but they served the function I required. So I hobbled and dragged my pregnant body around until I gave birth to a healthy bundle of joy. A son we called Brodie. He was of course adorable, and we loved him from the minute we saw him, just the same as we did our daughter Jasmine.

Now I had given birth I could at least get physiotherapy to try to heal and recover from the SPD. I was pushed and manipulated by several physiotherapists, to try to get my pelvis back into its original alignment. To no avail, I stayed twisted.

After about 6 months I went on to try Osteopathy, which gradually untwisted my pelvis over the course of a year. Just as it was almost straight, it shifted the other way, then pulled apart and stayed that way. That was when the pain got worse and shifted to my back as well as the front and right side of my pelvis.

You have no idea how much this hurt, and it only continued to get more and more painful by the day. At this point I gave up on a solution and resigned myself to a life of pain. My mum still looked though, and we went through a whole host of options, some of which helped, but not enough to make a difference to my quality of life.

So here I am on my kitchen floor, knife in hand. I was at the end of my tether. There were no more options available and I could not live like this anymore.

Then my son made a sound. He had been silent up until that point, so I had barely noticed him in my anguished state.

I looked up, straight into his eyes and just stared, captivated by my son's gaze. Something shifted in me. It was like I took a step out of time. Everything else faded away and it was like I could see the whole Universe in his eyes. It was an indescribable experience. Nothing mattered in that moment. There was only a profound stillness that stretched to eternity. It was so full of an exquisite still, silent presence that it was beyond words. My mind was blown away and the experience was all there was. Peace. A seemingly endless sea of peace and a silent wisdom, that was such a pure experience I could not look away. I was completely transfixed.

It had a hugely profound effect on me. There was hope. I didn't know what it was, but I knew there was hope. There was hope that things could change, that things could be different. Then my mind kicked in again and thoughts of what I had nearly done flooded in.

I was so ashamed that I had done this in front of my son. What effect would this have on him. I came to my senses. My husband saw the change in me and gently, but as swiftly as he dared, he took the knife from my grasp.

It was then, in that moment, that my whole life started all over again. I had to find a way to beat this. If I couldn't do it for myself, I could do it for my son. He was here after all. I was lucky to have him.

I felt the gratitude for the gift he was. I felt the love pouring out of his small, but powerful body. There was such innocence and trust that was so pure and clear. It was beautiful.

I could do this; I could find a way to be well and walk again. I had to at least try. I owed him this much. I chose to live. For my son, for my daughter, for my husband and most importantly, for myself.

I also wanted to find out what the transcendent experience was all about. If I could access an all-encompassing peace in such a distressing moment, surely I could find it again...

Chapter 2
Searching for a solution

I was ready to go again. To start a new search in order to find a solution to heal myself. With a new determination and thirst for results.

I had exhausted the conventional routes and so now I decided to think outside the box. I had experienced success in relieving the symptoms of ME using an alternative therapy called Reiki. So this was my first port of call.

I had been offered an operation from an Orthopaedic Surgeon to bolt a metal plate across the front of my pelvis to hold it together. Technically that sounded like a solution, except the Symphysis Pubis joint is meant to expand and contract when you move, stand up, sit down and even breathe. I was told I would feel the constriction and it would limit my movement. Well that didn't sound like fun. I was expected to accept that for the rest of my life. No thank you very much.

My dad, who was a Dentist and trusted the conventional world of medicine, wanted me to have the operation. He was very scared for me. So I promised to give the Reiki a chance and if I wasn't showing signs of improvement in 6 months, I would have the operation.

I actually had no intention of having the operation, so I was very motivated and determined that alternative approaches would work for me.

I started by having two Reiki treatments a week, as my condition was so acute. After the first treatment I could feel a bit of a difference, the pain was slightly less sharp and overwhelming, and I had a little more mobility. This was a huge relief for me. It may not have been much, but it was a promising start.

I continued having two treatments a week, until the pain had lessened to a degree that I could handle. Then I had one treatment a week for a while until I could move around more easily and the pain had reduced some more. Then the treatments were extended out to once a fortnight, then three weekly and then monthly.

By the time my promised six-month period had elapsed, I was actually just tentatively starting to walk again. This was amazing to both me and my dad. He was delighted to see me improve to such a great degree after being incapacitated and in agony for so long.

Along the way I had also discovered, (or rather my mum did), a support belt that I could strap around me, to relieve some of the pressure from the muscle and ligaments supporting my pelvis. This helped my recovery, as it took the strain, allowing my body to heal and re-balance itself naturally.

I was now walking again after over two years of disability. It was slow to begin with, but as the muscles in my legs adjusted to the exercise and movement, I grew stronger and more agile day by day. I started to live my life again.

As I was able to participate in more daily activities, I started to feel happier and less depressed. I was still in a fair amount of pain and I was also rather stiff and tense in most parts of my body. I was improving, but not fast enough for my liking. I knew there had to be more that I could do to continue the improvement and quality of life I currently experienced.

Reiki was great and had done so much for me. I was very grateful for having had the treatments that had given me a chance to participate in society again. But I was still limited, and my recovery had halted somewhat, so I began to look elsewhere for more help or inspiration to heal completely.

Chapter 3
A new journey begins

I devoured book after book on crystals, shamanism, living in the now, meditating and many more similar subjects. The books were great and very inspiring, but they didn't actually tell me how to live in the now, how to experience peace, or how to meditate effectively, just that it was possible and wonderful.

So I looked at ways to actually taste these experiences of peace and happiness. I found lots of workshops that promised just that. The workshops were very enjoyable and whilst I was on each workshop, I felt wonderful, happy, and excited to be alive. Then a few days to a week after the workshop had finished, it all faded away and I was anxious, angry, and depressed again.

There had to be a way to replicate the feeling I felt whilst I was at the workshops. To be able to have the experience in my everyday life. I continued to search and attended even more workshops. I met some lovely people, all searching for the same thing and started to swap books with one of the other course participants.

I was lent a book called 'First Thunder' by MSI. It was a novel about a man who discovered a group of people called the Ishayas, who taught him some techniques to experience peace and happiness and a greater level of enjoyment. It was similar to other books I had read, but somehow it spoke to me at a deeper level than anything else so far. It made sense beyond the understanding of my mind. I realised there was something about this story that resonated deep within me.

I searched for courses that would teach me the Ishayas' Ascension techniques. I found none. A year later my mum came to me with a website address, given to her from a friend who had learnt Ascension. It had the same name, so I looked it up and found that a course was happening in two weeks time. I suddenly felt unsure. I had been searching for this very course for a long time. But now it was presented to me, it felt a bit scary.

I left it until the next day when I looked on the website again. This time the course had moved location to a closer venue than before. It seemed like a sign, so I called the phone number advertised and booked a place on the course.

I felt ill the day before the course and I nearly talked myself out of going. But I am a determined person and knew I had to at least see whether it was going to be effective at helping me feel less pain and more peace. I had to give it a go.

I turned up at the venue and sat down in a chair and waited to see what would happen next. I looked around at the other course participants chatting away and it seemed like everyone knew each other. This made me feel alone and uncomfortable. However, as soon as the two teachers arrived and started talking, the discomfort fell away, and a profound sense of calm descended on me. I knew I was in the right place. I felt like I had arrived home.

The teachers were not only exceedingly happy and peaceful, they were also self-assured. I could see that they were clearly experiencing a much deeper level of contentment and enjoyment, than I had ever witnessed in anyone before. Whatever it was that they had, I knew I wanted it too. More than anything.

The course was inspiring, and I felt years of stress fall away in the one weekend. Much more beneficial and far reaching, than any other course I had attended prior to this one.

The real test though was when the weekend was over, and I was back in my everyday life again. Would this work away from the workshop environment? Nothing else had so far. I was nervous, but excited to try these techniques out at home.

I wasn't disappointed. They worked, they actually worked! I used them every day from that moment forward and the results have been absolutely incredible. The peace and calm growing in me, was far beyond anything I could have hoped for.

Even more importantly and exciting, is the Ascension techniques have continued to deliver. Each and every day since I learnt them, a greater and greater experience of peace, happiness and contented fulfilment has grown and expanded within me.

Not only have they worked to bring me to a direct experience of peace and calm. They have also given me more confidence and clarity. I see life completely differently now. It's like someone cleaned the world, cleared out the stress and created a brand-new place to live and explore.

Life was full and vibrant and so much more enjoyable. I started to do more, step up and join in with the 'parent teacher association' committee at my children's school. I started by just doing posters for them. As I grew in confidence, I became the secretary and then when the opportunity arose, I became the Chairperson and ran the whole committee.

I went on a car trial with my husband, something I would never have done before and certainly not enjoyed as much as I did. We were in an open top beach buggy, I had to navigate the whole day and it was freezing. We ended the day with a meal in a pub while we listened to the results and awards being handed out. I remember sitting there next to the fire shivering and trying to warm up. I felt happy and contented. I had enjoyed every moment, even with the discomfort of the cold and mud splattered all over my face. This was an entirely new way of experiencing life.

I still got stressed and anxious about things, but it happened less and less often, and the effects were vastly reduced. My health improved too. The pain eased off to a low level that I barely noticed anymore. I would get sick less often and the symptoms were less severe each time.

I was so impressed with these techniques and the teaching of the Bright Path Ishayas, that I started to have the desire to become a teacher myself.

That didn't seem possible though. The training course was six months in a retreat centre in Spain. I couldn't leave my husband and children for that long.

It was a long time before I dared voice this desire. It scared me, so I pushed the desire down and continued on with my life. Everything was easier anyway and I had started hosting courses for the Ishayas, so I was helping spread the teaching that way.

That was enough, wasn't it?

Well no, it wasn't…

Chapter 4
Leap of faith

I was hosting a course at my home, with a teacher who taught at the 'Mastery of the Self' retreat centre in Spain. He was Mexican and very direct with his words. While he was at my home, he asked me if I wanted to go on this retreat. An innocent enough question, to which I replied: "No, I can't leave my kids for that long". The teacher smiled and simply said "why not?".

My answer was not true. I had been harbouring a desire to become a teacher for several few months. But I was burying the desire to go, so this innocuous question sent my mind spinning out of control. I spent the whole of that night crying.

The next day my husband said: "You know you can go if you want to, I'll be fine looking after the kids on my own". This statement shocked me to the core. Then I realised, I was just using this as an excuse to avoid the truth of the matter. I was in fact afraid to be away from my home environment. Terrified actually. My heart wanted this more than anything, but my mind said no.

This went on for a couple of days. Until the pain of denying my desire, was worse than the fear of stepping outside my comfort zone. My heart finally won, and I chose to take a chance and do what I knew deep down, was what I was born to do.

I saw the teacher again the next day and told him I had decided to do it, to go to Spain for six months and become a teacher of Ascension. He smiled again and said, "My job is done".

Over the coming months, I dipped in and out of fear. Fear of going to Spain, fear of flying alone, fear of my family not coping without me. My mum was afraid for my children being without me. She was shocked that I would leave them for so long. She was also convinced that I was running away to join a cult and would either come home brainwashed or never return at all.

I'm not sure how a course to learn how to teach techniques that bring peace, can be confused with a cult. Plus, I was a rebel, I had never been good at doing anything that someone tried to push me to do or not do.

My choice to go remained unflinching, even when other parents said comments like: "You're leaving your children for how long?" Or "Is that a good idea to leave your kids alone?"

I wasn't actually leaving them on their own in any case. They had a Dad, a Nan and an Uncle living under the same roof. I still felt like I was doing something wrong, but I just had to go. I couldn't explain why, I just knew I had to. Things were better than they had been, but there was still plenty of room for improvement. I somehow knew that if I went, everything would be better. It would work out well in the end.

So I organised flights, currency, health insurance and everything else required for my extended stay. I couldn't quite commit to six months in the end, so I arranged to do the first three months of the course and intended to do the last three months the following year. This was a manageable amount of time for me to get my head around.

The time to go came around quickly, or so it appeared. I had somehow manifested a travel companion, so that helped with my fear of flying and travelling alone. Everything seemed to line up to support me in this adventure. This was a new experience for me. I was used to battling against life and having to try and force things to happen the way I would like. So the ease with which the arrangements were made, felt like a sign that this was the right path for me.

I felt emotional about leaving my husband and kids. They were brave when they waved me off in the airport, but I could see their sadness and worry hiding behind their smiles. I couldn't stop now though, so I walked through airport security and was on my way to Spain.

Walking away from my family was scary and I experienced a huge wave of emotion sweep over me. I was very grateful for Joanna, my newfound friend, who kindly chattered away to distract me from the overwhelming feeling of fear and loss.

It was a huge comfort to be with Joanna on the journey there. She wasn't just my travel companion, she was also a fellow 'leap of faith taker'. I would have done it without her, but I was grateful I didn't have to.

We finally arrived at the retreat centre at about 10pm at night. It was dark when the taxi dropped us outside the gates and then drove off into the night, leaving us alone up a mountain, on a Spanish hillside.

I suddenly realised the taxi had left and we weren't sure how to get into the retreat centre. There was nobody around, the gates were shut, with no obvious sign of entry. We both looked at each other in fright and I felt panic rising in me.

I looked around desperately seeking a solution, when I noticed what looked like a front door further up the hill from us. I dragged my suitcase up the hill to this door and knocked on it, praying it was the right place and they would understand English.

The door soon opened and a Mexican lady, who thankfully understood me well enough, found our name on the list. She took us to our accommodation and left.

Inside our room we found three other women, one was Australian and two other ladies who told us they were from Taiwan. They were so friendly and welcoming. We were able to rest at last and went to bed to see what the new day would bring us...

Chapter 5
Peace or pain

The following day we awoke to a glorious sunny day and the most beautiful view out over the mountainside, all the way down to the sea. The retreat centre was tranquil, so I felt instantly at home and safe in my new environment. I felt happy, apprehensive of what was ahead of me, but very content to be here at last.

The day was spent meeting people, meditating, and relaxing. It was all very easy. We got to listen to some amazing people talk about their experiences and I was feeling inspired and ready for the next three months, whatever it may hold.

I wasn't sure how I would ever become as peaceful, confident, and joyful as the teachers here so obviously were. I just crossed my fingers and hoped a miracle would happen and I would magically transform myself, into one of these teachers.

I was sitting, listening to someone speak and found myself enthralled with what was being said. Then the teacher in question said something I had never heard before. "Peace or Pain ... It's a choice." I was bewildered. "It's a choice?" I said silently in my head. It can't be, who would choose pain?

Well I knew I wouldn't choose for pain if there was a choice. But I was in pain and I didn't understand how I was choosing for it. The teacher then went on to explain that statement and although it made sense, I wasn't sure how that could, or would apply to me and my situation.

I went to dinner that day feeling happy and light-hearted. Over the course of the next few days, I enjoyed every moment. I was learning so much about myself and the patterns that I had played out my whole life. I discovered that these patterns were just something I had learnt and what I had learnt, I could unlearn.

I had a go at Yoga for the first time in years. I used to love practising Yoga before I had children. I used it throughout my first pregnancy and had an easy and smooth childbirth that time. Which I put down to the Yoga.

The next day I awoke to a sinking feeling in my stomach. When I got out of bed and walked to the bathroom, I found that my legs were weak, and it hurt to walk again. I was aghast, I had been recovering so well, I thought I would never have to face this pain or disability ever again.

I went to breakfast, hobbling all the way. I could walk, but only just and it took a lot of effort. I was feeling scared and disappointed ... and angry.

I managed as best I could, but when it came to walking up the hill to the meditation room, I had to keep stopping to catch my breath and summon the effort to continue walking.

I was devastated. I couldn't go through this again, I just hadn't the strength. It took all my will and determination to get to the top of the hill. When I got there, I had to sit down on the low wall at the top of the path. I leant against the railings with tears running down my face. Silently crying in desperation. I didn't know what to do. How would I manage to get around now? I may have to go home. I hadn't a clue what to do.

Then the words from the teacher ran through my mind. "Peace or Pain... It's a choice".

"Well" I thought vehemently in response, "if it's a choice ... I want Peace!"

And in that moment, the pain fell away and I was completely at peace with myself. I felt serene and stable, so I slowly stood up and walked into the meditation room.

I still found it awkward to walk, but I ceased to think about it. My mind was quiet and still. It was a beautiful experience and it stayed for quite some time.

Later that day I asked for help from one of the teachers. I told them how I was finding it difficult to walk and wasn't sure how I would manage being at the retreat centre if it didn't improve.

The next thing I knew, help was being offered from all sides. I was so well supported and helped in every way I needed. I had people to talk to about the frustration of the disability. There was a physiotherapist, who had specialised in my specific condition, five months prior to this course. He started giving me treatment sessions every few days. He also gave me a set of exercises to strengthen my muscles and retrain my body into a more natural alignment and improved posture.

Someone provided a stick to help me walk and the physiotherapist showed me how to use it more effectively. I was given Reiki and Remedial Massage to ease the physical effects. There was even an elderly gentleman who had a support belt he had brought for his back. He didn't need it, so he lent it to me to help to protect my pelvis and aid my ability to walk, along with the stick.

For a while I experienced no pain. But this was a new approach for me, and the pain sneaked back in. However, I now knew without a doubt that it was in fact a choice and one I continued to make with varying results. Once you know it is possible, as an experience, rather than just a concept, then you have hope. You have a method to keep choosing for. Old habits die hard, so it was a curious dance and a frustrating one at times. But one I was more than willing to make and continue to make.

Peace or Pain, I am delighted to report, is a real-life choice that anyone can make. Guidance is nearly always required, but it is available. If you want it … you'll find it.

Chapter 6
Finding myself

The following couple of months were a revelation. I started to discover who I really was, beyond all the limiting patterns that had ruled my life so far. I was given more Ascension techniques and each one uncovered another piece of the puzzle that was the 'real me'.

It became obvious, the closer I got to the end of the three months, that I wanted to continue and finish the six months this year. It was a challenge for my husband and my kids to hear that. They may have been happy to start off with, but they missed me more than they expected, and it was harder for one parent to do it all and work as well.

I changed my mind several times. I wanted to stay, but my husband was not coping on his own. It was a lot to ask. After a Skype call with my husband, in which he said he couldn't do it any longer. I gave up hope. I messaged him to say don't worry, I'll come home as planned at the end of the three months.

I then put my phone down and walked out of my room. There standing in front of me was my husband, with backpack and a sheepish smile.

He missed me so much, he just booked a ticket and got on a plane and turned up without telling me. It was a clear 10 seconds before I recognised who he was! He didn't look any different, but I was not expecting him to just show up, so my mind couldn't make sense of what I was seeing.

The two days he was there with me, were a roller coaster of emotion for us both. My mind did not know what to think! It was uncomfortable, but also very freeing. He left happier, but the plan was for me to still come home.

I wasn't content with this, but it was good to see him and it wasn't fair to pressure him, if he wasn't willing. So I let it go and continued on with the course for as long as I had left.

The last few weeks went by fast. I felt wonderful, but the desire to stay just got stronger and stronger. I got up the courage and asked my husband again if I could stay. I could come home for a couple of weeks in the middle to see him and the children. Then return to complete the last three months.

To my surprise he agreed. It wasn't going to be easy for him. But I knew deep down that if I did this now, everything would work out. And if I didn't ... well I didn't want to think about not doing it at all.

So I got to stay. My husband struggled, but managed. It was hard on the children. I was harshly judged by other parents. But I knew this was the right thing to do in the long run.

In the second three months, I gave it my all. I was focused and determined to prove it was worth the sacrifices my family were making, so that I could finish the course.

I released huge amounts of stress from my nervous system and my experience became more and more stable as each day went by. I was continually amazed at how different life could be.

My perception changed and changed again, as I was shown time and time again, that I was valuable. I could now access a vast wealth of knowledge and directly experience a deep stable connection to an inner strength, wisdom and peace that had been there all along. I had missed it, because I had too much stress and emotional attachment to my thoughts, which clouded my perception of everything that was said to me or done around me.

By the end of the six months, I was feeling very secure and serene. I was a totally different person, yet I hadn't changed at all. I was more myself than I had ever been. It felt like I could do anything and be myself, no matter what went on around me.

It was almost as if I had received a deep cleansing. All my sorrows were washed away. The world was lighter and brighter, much more exciting and enjoyable for me.

I graduated as a Bright Path Ishaya Teacher. I was a little nervous about teaching, but I had a renewed enthusiasm to show others what was possible. If I could do it, then so could anyone.

I had transformed from the anxious, nervy little mouse into an empowered, strong, and confident person. It was little short of a miracle. I would not have believed it possible if I hadn't experienced it for myself.

It was everything I had hoped for and more. I had seen others achieve this state and I had desired it for a long time. But nothing compared to the actual direct experience of becoming that for myself.

I had gone from the concept of peace, to the direct experience of peace. Peace is an alive, vibrant, and very enjoyable state of being. I now understood why the eyes of other Ishaya Teachers were so lit up. It's like a beautiful light reveals itself and shines from you. You can't always see it, but you can definitely feel it.

You could say I found my Self. I was experiencing life from the authentic, free flowing experience of my true, original, and pure state of being. Life was much more clear, simple, and easy, lived from this state. It was much more pleasant than the cluttered, stressful, strained existence which I had previously experienced. I had believed I was not important and had no idea that there was another choice. Another way to live your life. Another way to be.

By the time I left the retreat centre, I was able to walk unaided again. The pain had also dramatically reduced. I wasn't 100% healed, but I was physically able with just a few occasional aches and pains.

Thank goodness for The Bright Path Ishayas and the practice of Ascension. It gave me my life back, my freedom and the ability to choose for peace. I was able to choose for a life without any limitation. Without the need to judge and second guess my every move. All I had to do was make the choice and keep making the choice for peace.

And this was only the beginning!

Now I could begin to create a life that was fulfilling and rewarding. Enjoyable and exciting. Peaceful and enlivening all at the same time. I was, at long last, free to be me!

My family were delighted to have me home with them and very much enjoyed the new 'me'. They were all very stressed on my return though and there were a few issues to address. However, their sense of relief was palpable, and they soon relaxed when they saw how peaceful I had become.

It was strange to be living with my family again, but I was so much more relaxed and able to take everything in my stride. It felt easy to fit back into everyday life. My experience of peace was incredibly stable, and this radiated out to my family as well.

It was the greatest gift of all, to be able to share this peace with my loved ones.

Chapter 7
A brave new world

I started teaching Ascension and it was always a beautiful experience. Every weekend course I taught was not only a privilege, it was also a delight and hugely beneficial for my own experience too.

Watching people as they turned up on the Friday evening, stressed and apprehensive was a little nerve-racking at first. What if I couldn't have the impact I desired? I was often very tired by the end of the first evening. But as I continued to teach and got to see people relax over the course of the weekend, leaving with smiles and a renewed sense of joy for life, it got easier and easier.

This really works! I already knew this of course from my own experience. But to see others grow and lighten up and realise they could experience peace so easily, was a whole new level of wonderful.

This is who I am, who I've always been. To help others and show them what is actually possible and how simple and easy it can be, has been and still is very fulfilling.

My pain went away completely, and I felt amazing. As time went on and life just got better and better, I thought this is it, I'm free!

This is a dangerous thought to have, as I soon found out. Being free involves no thinking about how well or not you are doing. I did know this theoretically, but I hadn't yet quite realised how much thinking was still going on behind the scenes in my unconscious mind.

There was still a subtle idea of stopping thoughts or just ignoring them and they'll go away, playing in my mind. This is not how it works in reality, so I was heading for another wake up call. Although I had no pain as such, my body would still feel heavy and tired on waking each morning. I also had aches and strains that popped up every now and then.

There were still occasions when I was triggered though, and I would feel angry for apparently no reason. Or some small insignificant situation would make me feel furious out of the blue.

I didn't realise it at the time, but I was still repressing a lot of emotion and my body was starting to show signs of stress.

For a few years I carried on in this way. It felt ok, good even, because I was continually feeling more peaceful and joyful. Life was pretty fulfilling and enjoyable, easy and calm. So all was well.

I was becoming more confident as I stepped out of my comfort zone again and again. All seemed to be ticking along nicely.

I was planning another trip to the retreat centre in Spain. I went every year as a visiting teacher to 'plug into the mains'. Each time I went back, I would stabilise my peace even more and return feeling refreshed and vibrant.

I was very much looking forward to going again this year. This was the first time I was attending a retreat just for teachers and I was excited to be spending three weeks there instead of the usual two.

I arrived with a few other teachers from the UK and was delighted to be back to explore some more with an amazing group of conscious and happy people.

The first few days were such a joy! I was feeling rested and free. There were many teachers from around the world that I already knew, and I enjoyed catching up with them all in person. There were also plenty of teachers I hadn't met before and it was lovely to chat and get to know them too.

I had been doing a specific yoga routine and continued with the same practice every morning. It was nice to be able to practice alongside my friends each day.

On about the fifth day of the retreat, however, everything changed. I went down to the meeting room to practice my usual yoga routine and felt a little stiff and sore. I thought nothing of it to start with, although there was a feeling of unease that was hovering just at the edge of my awareness.

I started my routine and my legs just wouldn't do the usual stretches. Very quickly I realised my Symphysis Pubis joint was not working properly. It had happened so many times before, so it was something I recognised straight away.

I couldn't believe it. My heart sank and I felt distraught. No, no, no, not again surely? But it was happening again and this time it was a complete relapse.

I hobbled back to my room and cried. This was not supposed to happen. I had healed myself to a really good level of health and fitness.

By breakfast time, I could hardly walk at all. My lovely roommates took it in turns to bring me food, whilst I stayed in my bed resting and practicing my Ascension techniques.

I was shocked and angry and was only just keeping tears at bay.

Everyone around me was so kind and did whatever I needed to help me get around, so I could still join in with the retreat. Some of the men would stand either side of me, so I could lean on them to hobble down to the meeting room, which was thankfully near my room. It's really hard work moving around when you can't lift your legs.

After a couple of days, a pair of crutches materialised from a previous participant and I managed to move around on my own again. But as anyone who has had to use crutches will tell you, it is not easy to go everywhere on crutches. My hands were sore from leaning on the handles and I was exhausted from the effort of moving around.

The worst part was my state of mind though. I felt useless and full of despair. Thoughts piled in about how long it will go on for and what if this is it for the rest of my life, etc.

I was not the usual happy and contented person I had been for the last seven years. It was then that I realised, as I acknowledged my misery, how much emotion was overwhelming me. Then it swiftly followed that I remembered I had a choice - peace or pain?

Even if I couldn't walk, I could still choose for peace now. That choice was always available, I just had to choose. Now when something like this flares up and emotion overwhelms you, it's difficult to just choose. But I knew it was possible and I had so many people around me to remind me to make the choice and keep making it.

From that moment I lightened up and started to see the funny side of things again. As I stopped taking everything so seriously, my state of mind changed.

I was able to become more aware of stillness and keep choosing for that. The more I remembered the more I was reminded to choose for peace and allow everything to happen as it was happening.

The fight in me fell away and I was at peace once more.

Physically I still needed help, but that turned out to be lovely, once I allowed myself to receive the help. I got to spend more time with more people, who I may not have got to know so well if this hadn't happened.

I was constantly blown away by how kind everyone was and how much fun it was to interact with them whilst they were helping me. I stopped feeling isolated and self-obsessed and started enjoying every moment exactly as it was presented to me.

Then magic started to reveal itself. Someone lent me a support belt so I could move around more easily. Another teacher, who was also an Alexander technique teacher, showed me how to move more freely, without activating my postural habits.

I received free massages and other treatments which kick started healing and made me feel a lot more stable on my feet. I could now lift my legs a little and that made life physically a lot easier.

But the most magical experience of all, was my body became able to do more with less effort. As I played and explored the stillness, allowed everything that happened to happen and flow through me, my body became more flexible and stronger.

It was a moment by moment choice. One moment I would feel heavy and struggle to move. The next I was able to move freely and easily and the symptoms appeared to have gone.

So much emotion flowed through me and it was still overwhelming at times, because I was resisting before I realised what I was doing. But I kept choosing and doing whatever I needed to do to look after my body.

I was hoping the flare up would subside before I left the retreat, but that was not to be. I was wondering how I was going to get home and contemplating ordering a wheelchair. Then the lovely teacher who lent me his support belt, came and told me I could keep it to travel home in. It was his gift to me.

I was so touched and beyond grateful! The kindness of such a beautiful soul made me cry. Although this time it was tears of joy and gratitude.

I made my way home with the hope that the flare up would heal up soon. Surely it would make a difference when I had my memory foam mattress and home comforts.

This was also not to be. I had to find a way to accept my current physical state and work with my new level of immobility.

Chapter 8
Making the best of things

It was a bit tricky to begin with; adjusting to life wearing a support belt wherever I went and no longer being able to lift anything heavier than a kettle.

Life went on as usual and I found ways to get around my disability. I was grateful for many things though. The main one being I was still able to put my own socks on and dress myself this time.

I am a creative and resourceful person, so I approached it all with a light heart and a determination to find another way to carry out my daily tasks. Most things were still possible and for everything else, I had to get good at asking for help again!

I was so grateful for the stability in my inner experience. I was nearly always able to recognise that peace was present. When I forgot, I chose again as soon as I recognised, I was battling against the status quo.

The only thing that kept me going when emotion overwhelmed me, was a deep sense of this being the chance to move past this condition once and for all. I wasn't sure how, but I was convinced this was coming up to be healed.

The recognition of presence and the ability to choose for it each and every day, has been my saving grace. I cannot even imagine what it would be like to not have this ability to choose.

The strength of spirit that has always risen in me when adversity calls, arose again and fortified me. If it was possible to transcend this state, then I was willing to explore and play until I found a way.

This is no longer a fight for me though. The way forward is to allow and work with everything that presents in my daily life.

My role as an Ishaya monk is the foundation for every decision I make and provides me with an ongoing experience of peace that is the solid ground required to move through life with ease and grace.

I made sure to remain alert and focused on being present, so the best course of action or non-action could be recognised as it came to me and through me.

I had already started writing this book and this gave me the project that inspired me to keep exploring and stay open to what serves me best in each and every moment.

I already knew how to transcend pain, so it was important to me that I found a way to share this knowledge and experience with the world.

I had been waiting to be completely healed before I completed the book. But along the way I have realised life is a continual exploration of more. We think we want an end result, but in reality, we really want and need to continually grow and expand our experience of this moment. As human beings we need new experiences and variety to stay fulfilled and contented.

As I explored my experience of stillness, so my body softened and relaxed. I stopped approaching my Symphysis Pubis condition as something to get rid of. Instead I explored what was possible now and worked with what I could do. All the while focusing on being present first and foremost.

I am constantly amazed at how much tension I have held for so long in every part of my body. Until it started falling away, I had no idea how much tension I had been storing all these years.

My legs and arms can often have a pins and needles sensation as they start to relax and release all the stored stress. Sometimes it's a pleasant tingling sensation and sometimes I feel a burning sensation that feels uncomfortable. I prefer the tingling sensation of course. But I've learnt to allow it all and not judge whether it's good or bad. It just is.

Resistance will make it feel worse, so I allow it all and do whatever occurs to me to do. Whether that's to exercise and strengthen my body so it can become fit and healthy. Or rest and relax to allow my body to rebalance and release the tension.

The biggest turning point for me was in 2020, when the Covid 19 virus closed the whole world and lock down began. Most people were depressed and afraid, but I was grateful for the opportunity to slow down and stop the daily activities that were pushing my Symphysis Pubis joint to its limits.

Only two weeks after lock down began, I was able to take my support belt off and begin to walk unaided after nearly a year of wearing it.

I felt incredibly vulnerable at first, but I knew that this is a good place to be. So I accepted the feeling and gradually explored gentle exercise to rebuild my muscle strength.

One of the most valuable things for me has been serving others. I host online meetings and one to one sessions to help others experience peace. Some are with people who experience pain, and some are with those who just want to reduce stress and experience more peace.

I also started doing talks in March 2020. The theme of the talks is changing your relationship with pain. Peace is always possible and I'm making that my ongoing reality and helping others do the same.

The fear I have felt all my life has fallen away and that has made a dramatic difference. I feel safe and that means I am able to open up and be myself.

I am currently in no pain and can walk unaided with no problem. My muscle strength is building back up and I feel lighter and more comfortable in my posture and movement. I no longer need to be completely healed to be at peace. My body follows my mental state, so I do not suffer at all and healing happens all by itself.

As I finish this book, I am happy and contented with everything in my life. Challenges arise, but I relish them now and simply allow the energy to move, so I can remain still and present.

Do you want a life like this too?

Then read on and explore the second, third and fourth parts of this book to find out how to begin changing your relationship with pain.

Part Two
Understanding Pain

"As long as you make an identity for yourself out of the pain, you cannot become free of it. As long as part of your sense of self is invested in your emotional pain, you will unconsciously resist or sabotage every attempt that you make to heal that pain. Why?

Quite simply because you want to keep yourself intact, and the pain has become an essential part of you. This is an unconscious process, and the only way to overcome it is to make it conscious.

"The pain-body, which is the dark shadow cast by the ego, is actually afraid of the light of your consciousness. It is afraid of being found out. Its survival depends on your unconscious identification with it, as well as on your unconscious fear of facing the pain that lives in you. But if you don't face it, if you don't bring the light of your consciousness into the pain, you will be forced to relive it again and again."

- Eckhart Tolle -

Chapter 9
The choice between peace and pain

When this question was first posed to me, I was shocked. I hadn't even known there was a choice. I had been in pain, or had some health condition, illness, or discomfort with my body, for as long as I could remember. So there I was, being told it was in fact a choice and one we continually make in each and every moment.

This idea of there being a choice can be challenging if, like me, you have been in pain, have a serious health condition or have been ill for a long time. But it <u>is</u> a choice and when I first found this out, I chose to believe, or rather hope that this was true. The pain wasn't that bad for me in that exact moment of discovery. However, as I said in an earlier chapter, I soon had the chance to explore if there was any truth behind these words.

It's an obvious choice for most people to want peace instead of pain. But how do you make that choice?

The first step is to find out it is possible, and the second step is to hope or believe it is true. You then need to find out how to make the choice and be willing to do whatever it takes to make the choice.

Persistence is also necessary, so you keep making the choice, in the face of evidence that tells you it's not possible. I know it appears as if your pain is fixed and you have no way out. But this is not true, you have just got stuck in a pattern which is keeping you in a state of pain and suffering.

So how do we change this pattern we have become accustomed to? It has a lot to do with where you put your attention in any given moment.

We have learnt to put our attention on the outside world. We rely on other people and their opinions to tell us how we are doing, or what we should be doing. We focus on the situations that happen in our life and on what material possession we have, or other people have.

We have lost touch with our self and have become dependent on other people to validate us. We put our self-worth on how much money we earn and what possessions we have. We have learnt to take things personally. If something happens that we don't like it hurts us, whether that is physical, mental, or emotional pain. We have learnt this means we have done something wrong, or somebody else has done something wrong.

We have allowed these external things to define us. To affect our every waking moment, until we are overwhelmed to the point of breaking. Then we pick ourselves up, lecture ourselves and repeat the pattern all over again.

This is not good for our health. Not just physical health, but mental and emotional health. We become out of balance and ineffective in our actions and words. We become more and more tense and rigid, in everything we say and do. Our body becomes dense, heavy and inflexible. This means our health deteriorates. Whether it is just headaches, or colds, or more permanent conditions, such as allergies and a whole host of diagnosed conditions.

It also has a lot to do with whether you are resisting or allowing.

When you are resisting life, resisting emotions, resisting your thoughts, resisting what people say to you, resisting situations and events, you are causing yourself to suffer. Resistance always leads to suffering.

Resistance also limits abundance in the form of money, love, happiness, good health, and anything you have ever wanted.

Resistance causes the tension and pain you wish to avoid. Until you stop resisting, you will continue to experience stress, pain and suffering in all forms.

Peace is a natural, happy, healthy state of being. Our original operating mode so to speak. It is accessible now, within us and all you have to do to access it, is find a technique, a vehicle, to take you to that still, silent space within to experience it directly.

Peace or Pain is a choice we make every day, unconsciously without realising. You can change this and make that choice a conscious one in each and every moment. Then you can change your relationship with pain.

It can be a gradual process, because the habit to resist and put our attention on the outside is a strong one. But it can also be a fast, almost instantaneous change.

In reality we are in a state of peace every time we stop resisting for a moment, or we choose for a technique. But it doesn't always feel that way, because the habit kicks back in so fast and we are lost in another thought created reality. Peace can be so fleeting that we miss it, we don't consciously experience it. But if you can commit to changing this and be persistent, then the changes will happen. Peace can become your everyday consciously recognised reality. You may leave this for pain occasionally, until the habit completely falls away. Then all that is left is peace.

It is not a linear process either. Sometimes it can feel like you are going backwards, or nothing has changed at all. This is because you are releasing the stresses stored, from a lifetime of habitual thinking patterns and resistance. When you are releasing these stresses, your attention can be reduced from everything in your awareness to just the thought, emotion or pain that is being released. Then it can be intense or overwhelming and you suffer. However, with persistence, the stress will fully release, and peace can be consciously recognised again.

Peace is only ever experienced now. Thinking about peace may seem and feel positive, but thinking requires energy, which causes stress in our body. Thinking also takes us away from the present moment. If you are thinking, you can only ever be in a mind created version of the past, or a mind created version of the future.

The body always responds to and mirrors the ideas playing out in the mind. Even a positive subject, such as peace, can cause stress to be stored. This is because the very fact you are thinking about peace, means you are not in the actual experience of peace. If you were experiencing peace, you would just rest in the presence of peace and have no need to think about it, or look elsewhere.

Most thinking happens because of a belief there is something wrong, or something missing. It's simply an idea something needs to be fixed or changed, playing out in our unconscious mind. Like a record playing on repeat.

Thinking is a problem-solving tool we need only use when there is something which needs planning, arranging, or solving in that moment. Solutions usually happen as flashes of inspiration when we have given up and thinking has stopped momentarily. We don't need to use the mind as often as we think we do!

Most thinking is unnecessary and therefore takes us away from our naturally, still, restful state of being. In order to think we have to leave the present moment and remember the past or project into the future. All thinking is conceptual. It is not real. But what we think about, we feel as emotions and physical sensations in the body. Therefore, it feels real.

Because it feels real, we keep focusing on it, believing it to be real. What we put our attention on, we experience. Either as a feeling, or a state of being. We are either living in a pure state of being, or we are living in a perceived state of reality, based on our internal commentary.

Both feel real, so it can be difficult to discern the difference. However, if you use a technique to put your attention within and start to directly experience peace, it becomes more tangible and recognisable. With your attention on peace, the body naturally releases stress from the nervous system and thinking slows down and stops. You become a master of your mind, rather than a victim to the overwhelming, never ending stories and opinions that drown you in the feelings which are then generated.

To master the mind is very easy, with effective meditation techniques and guidance. Guidance is a crucial part of the process. This is because the mind is very clever at impersonating a peaceful state, by creating a peaceful feeling. It is easy to get lost in that feeling and this will keep the mind in play. It can also complicate everything and make it seem like you have to keep thinking positively, to stay in this pleasant state of feeling peaceful.

Peace is a natural state, so the mind can trick you into thinking that because it is natural, you don't need to do anything to experience it, therefore meditation techniques are not required. Nor is any guidance for the same reason.

Peace is a state which is beyond all thinking. Any thinking takes us away from peace. There are many mind traps that can persuade you to stop using meditation techniques or asking for guidance.

The mind does not want to give up control. It has become the master and it doesn't want to stop. The meditation techniques threaten that control. We have become so identified with the mind, that it persuades us <u>we</u> are making the choice. The mind will decide the process of meditation is not necessary to be free and at peace.

Guidance provides a light, to show the way through all these pitfalls in the mind. Allowing us to keep practising meditation to stabilise and strengthen this natural peaceful state of being. Eventually the mind loses its power of persuasion and we can more easily discern the traps for ourselves.

Then we can remain in an eternal, perpetual state of peace, happiness, and freedom. That is our birthright.

Chapter 10
What is pain?

Let's take a closer look at what pain really is, beyond our conceptual understanding and past experience of it. Pain is simply a signal from a part of the body to the brain. <u>This signal is to alert us that part of our body needs our attention.</u>

It may be help is required, for example if we have been cut and are bleeding, we may need to take action to stop the blood flowing from us. Or we may be doing an action which is damaging us in some way, like hitting our thumb with a hammer, or running when the muscles need a rest. In these cases, we can stop what we are doing and if necessary, look after the damaged, or hurt part of us.

But long-term pain is a little different. It is still a signal, which means our attention is required. But our body does not necessarily need us to do anything. We may just need to pay attention, to place our attention on the part of us which hurts. To become present in the body.

For example, a common long-term pain is felt in the lower back, neck, or shoulders. When you place 100% of your attention on the painful body part, just watch and wait. It gives the body a chance to heal, balance and adjust itself, to redress what is causing the pain. Sometimes all that is needed, is to just simply relax and release the tension held there.

With long term pain we also need to stop what is causing the pain. Similar to the hammer example. But in this case, it is not obvious we are doing anything. So, the conclusion is then there is something wrong with this body part.

And that is a possibility. But more often than not, our body just needs us to pay attention to it. Then we can receive any information the body may be trying to tell us. With back pain it is common our posture is not natural any longer and an unnatural posture puts pressure on areas which are not meant to be pressured.

The body is trying to alert you to this fact. But postures change very gradually, and we are often not aware we have started to hunch our shoulders or tense one leg, which then begins to twist the spine. When I first learnt my spine was twisted, I didn't know why or how.

We have spent a long time tensing little bit by little bit and do not notice how far we have twisted and bent our body out of its natural shape. If you look around you in a public place, you will notice a lot of people, from a very young age, are bent over at the shoulders. It has almost become normal looking, because so many people have this curved shape now.

But it is most definitely not normal and is, I believe, the reason why back pain of some sort is so common in society these days.

I didn't realise how twisted I was until I went to see an osteopath. I was told I had one leg longer than the other and I had scoliosis with one hip higher than the other. I have since found out that I do not have one leg longer than the other, but that my posture had changed to create this effect, by tensing itself on one side of my body. My spine was twisted and curved, but it is not a fixed condition that I was born with. It has happened over time because of muscles tensing either side of my spine in different areas which have twisted and curved my spine out of its natural position.

I have now become much more aware of the habits I have learnt which tense and reshape my body. I have become aware of unnatural movements that are unconscious and harmful. Once you discover what you are doing to cause the unnatural posture, you can start to reprogram these habits to more healthy and comfortable ones.

. . .

But that is only one type of pain. There are plenty of others attributed to a whole host of different health conditions.

One thing I've learnt from researching pain has been it's not necessarily just physical.

Pain often, if not always, has an emotional element. It can even be the sole cause of the pain, or illness we are experiencing. I'll go into more details about emotions in a later chapter.

For now, I will talk more about what is the actual cause of pain we feel in our body.

In treating the process of observation like a scientific experiment, I have discovered a lot of information I would never have discovered, had I not stopped to pay attention to my body.

For a start, I noticed when I just paused for a moment and observed the part of my body which was in pain or discomfort, (from a neutral standpoint) it often softened, and the pain eased. In some cases, it went away completely.

This was a huge revelation and I became fascinated by what was occurring and how I could use this experiential feedback to transform the current state of my body.

Then I read a book by Dr John Sarno called Healing Back Pain. In this book he explains that the actual cause of pain is a lack of oxygen. The lack of oxygen was caused by tension, held in the area of the body that was felt as painful.

So why do we hold tension in the body?

Well, for me it comes back to what activity is going on in the mind. We are literally tensing against the negative thoughts which are incessantly flowing through our mind. I have discovered by paying attention, (as part of my meditation practice) I notice tension somewhere in my body. I also began to notice I was actually thinking at the same time.

Just by becoming aware of this, resulted in the thinking ceasing. This is because the light of conscious awareness naturally dispels the unconscious thinking pattern. Just as when a light is turned on in a dark room, the darkness instantly disappears.

What happens next, is what trips us up again and again.

When we cease thinking and are consciously aware and alert, all the stored stresses start to release. As part of the release of stress stored in our nervous system, we may experience a whole host of different symptoms and feelings.

If we surrender to this process, then all the movement of feeling and body sensations are gentle and easy. We may not even notice them at all.

But more often than not we resist this process. We resist the release of stress because it feels uncomfortable. In fact, resistance is something we've been trained to do from an early age. It's so deeply ingrained. We actually resist first and then the discomfort follows. It's just an unconscious process, so we don't know it is happening.

We were trained to resist to fit into the idea of society we were born into. When we cried, we were told 'It's okay, don't cry' or something similar. Our caregivers did everything to try to stop us expressing our pain, frustration, sadness, or hurt.

Or maybe we were ignored if we expressed our feelings, so we learnt to stop if we wanted attention. The same with anger. I was often told to calm down when I was frustrated or angry. The perceived injustice or unfairness was never addressed, so I learnt to internalise the feeling.

Whatever our childhood experience was like, pretty much everybody has some story about how they were not allowed to feel the way they were feeling at some point. In trying to understand the world around us, we learnt certain responses were wrong or not acceptable.

I always remember feeling bewildered and confused, as every natural impulse I had was stopped. I was gradually trained to fit into, initially my parents, then schoolteachers and other adults view of the world.

I found this very difficult. I never understood or related to what I was being told. It made no sense to me whatsoever.

However, I gradually learnt to curtail my natural impulses and respond in the way I was expected to. The only problem was, because I didn't understand the rules I often got into trouble for my words and actions. This meant I withdrew from the world more and more. I started to live in a state of fear, in fight, flight or freeze mode.

I had no idea what was expected of me most of the time, so I stopped speaking unless I was sure of the result, or someone insisted on an answer. I often got the answer they were expecting wrong and was told off, humiliated, laughed at or punished.

This resulted in me either saying nothing, or blurting out whatever my mind could conjure up. Meantime I became more and more resentful, with no outlet for this resentment. I became a very angry individual, very easily triggered, when I could no longer contain my feelings.

After a dramatic and chaotic experience at primary school, I learnt to manage my outbursts by the time I went to secondary school. I became extremely introverted and shy.

I began to identify with this and eventually decided that a shy introvert was just my personality. I've since discovered this is not true. It was just the way I learnt to be, so I could avoid as much confrontation as possible.

Your story may be very different, but you get the idea? We learnt to resist, so we could fit in, stay safe, be liked and accepted by our fellow human beings, young and old.

. . .

Resistance and repression have therefore become an ingrained habit, which effects every area of our life, especially pain.

From the moment I first discovered there was a choice between peace and pain, I have been told by Ishaya teachers to allow the pain to be there.

This is easier said than done.

However, before I heard this idea of a choice being available to me, I had a profound experience of allowing.

I was on a 10-day retreat in Oxfordshire with The Bright Path Ishayas. It was run by two of the mastery course teachers Satta and Narain. I came on the retreat because I had already met Narain at a course near where I lived and he was so gentle and kind, yet so direct with a very powerful presence. I wanted to experience what he had.

I was ascending in the afternoon one day, about halfway through the retreat and I was in a lot of physical pain. The pain had been with me since lunchtime and it just seemed to be intensifying with every Ascension technique I used. It was becoming more and more unbearable, so I got up from my chair to find Narain to help me. When I say help, what I really wanted was for him to take the pain away from me.

I wandered into the main area where Narain was usually hanging around, so he could be available if we needed help or guidance. Narain was nowhere to be seen, so I just stood there uncertain of what to do next.

Then a teacher called Garuda, who I had never met before, approached me to ask if he could help me. I didn't know him and really wanted Narain, but I was desperate, so I said, "yes please".

We sat down to one side and he asked me how he could be of service. I blurted out this pain in my forehead was excruciating, it just seemed to be building up and up and I could not bear it any longer.

Garuda looked at me with a kind, gentle smile and asked me "Can you let the pain be there just for a moment"?

I wanted to scream at him:

"NO! That's why I asked for help, I want the pain to go away".

But instead, as I looked back into his eyes which exuded kindness, compassion, and a stillness beyond comprehension, I found myself replying "Ok".

In that moment the pain vanished, completely and utterly vanished and I experienced a warm, gentle, soothing yet powerful energy flowing throughout my whole body, emanating from my heart. I just blinked and was silent because there were no words.

Nothing could explain the experience I was having in that moment. It was profound and beautiful and totally blew me away.

When the experience calmed down and I was still in no pain whatsoever, I just said to Garuda "What just happened? Did you see that"?

He smiled at me and said something like "Yes I saw it. It looked like your heart opened up and expanded." I could see he was moved by what he had witnessed. Which was a relief in a way, because it meant I hadn't imagined it.

I thanked him and went back to ascend with no further pain, just witnessing and experiencing this beautiful softness with gentle energy continually flowing through me.

I thought I had mastered pain there and then! But alas it was only the beginning of a frustrating dance between allowing and there being no pain, versus allowing so the pain would go away. It may seem like a subtle difference, but the experience is worlds apart.

I learnt bit by bit to allow the pain to be there. It softened whenever I managed to be surrendered enough to let the energy flow through me, rather than to resist, put up a battle and want it gone. But it seemed to be a tricky dance, because of course I always wanted the pain to go. It was difficult to allow the pain when it was so intense and uncomfortable.

It's a dance I am still doing, but with much more success. This is because I am becoming more and more alert. I can therefore see much more clearly, when I am thinking, or tensing against the movement of energy passing through my conscious awareness.

I don't battle with it anymore and consequently don't experience so much pain. And when I do experience pain, it is just a signal to stop the fight, to stop thinking and instead simply pay more attention, allowing everything to happen without trying to control the experience.

What I have discovered during the past few years is, it is only when I am unaware of what I am doing that I experience any pain at all.

What I mean by this is, over my lifetime I learnt to hold back my natural impulses. Holding back is actually something I am doing which requires effort. To try to not be yourself, is something most of us have learnt to do. In order to fit in to society, we have curbed our natural instincts, so we are acceptable to others.

This is such a soul-destroying thing to do. Not to mention the fact it requires a lot of energy.

In my experience, it is this holding back of our natural impulses which leads to pain occurring in the first place.

Our body is actually always trying to rebalance, to come back to its natural healthy state of being. But because we have learnt to resist this natural flow, we stop our body from functioning effectively and efficiently, causing it to malfunction and operate under continual strain.

It has been fascinating to discover pain is not what I thought it was. To experience first-hand how my relationship with pain can be different, if I allow my body to operate unhindered.

Another example of how different your experience can be is best illustrated by the exploration I did when I broke my ribs a few years ago.

The same situation of having broken ribs was experienced in two completely different ways.

The first way, that most of us would experience and expect to experience, was a world of pain and suffering. I could hardly move without being winded and experiencing a sharp, extremely intense stab of pain. This would happen when I moved too fast, or in a way that my body didn't want to move, in order to protect itself from further damage.

I could not lie down for many weeks and so sleep was restless and intermittent. Very early on in this situation I remembered pain was a choice. Rather than be frustrated when I was experiencing pain and therefore my mind deemed me as failing, I decided to make it a game. So I began a gentle experiment to discover what was possible, what made a difference to my experience and what did not.

I obviously don't recommend broken ribs, but it was a very interesting and insightful experience. The more I was light and playful in my approach, the more successful the results were.

I could go from excruciating pain in one moment, when I was resisting and wanting my experience to be different from what it was right now. To the next moment, when I paid full attention and allowed my body to be exactly as it was right now. Then my experience changed dramatically to a completely gentle and alive one. An experience in which I was aware of the site of my broken and cracked ribs, yet there was no pain, just a body sensation, that was neither pleasant nor unpleasant.

Strangely in this surrendered state of allowing, I was able to move much more easily and with a greater range of movement as well.

It was fascinating to witness the differences. It was obviously a much nicer experience when I was allowing than when I was resisting. As time went on, I got much more proficient in being able to access and remain in this state of being.

Since that time, I have had many more realisations which have led me to an entirely different approach to life. At some point I recognised it wasn't a case of allowing the pain, which no-one wants to do anyway because it hurts. It was in fact more beneficial to allow the natural movement of healing in the body.

This new, more gentle approach is much easier to sustain and made much more sense to me. To allow pain is counterintuitive, whereas to allow healing to take place, is supporting a desirable outcome to manifest. Of course, it makes more sense to simply rest back and watch my body rebalance all by itself and begin to operate more effectively and efficiently!

Pain becomes more understandable the more you pay attention and stop interfering. This is because you get to see how useful pain is and that it is a necessary part of human experience.

Pain is simply a way of getting our attention when we are doing something which is harmful to us, so we can ensure we are operating in a more holistic and harmonious way.

One thing I've learnt and had hammered home recently is, until we learn to fully allow emotion to flow through us unhindered, we will cause harm to our bodies and we will suffer.

Suffering, by the way, only happens when we resist 'what is'.

Allowing means everything works harmoniously. Resisting means we interrupt the natural process of energy passing through and enlivening our body.

Pain is always a possibility, not inevitable but it is a possibility.

Suffering however, is not necessary at all.

I'll say it again because it's worth repeating.

SUFFERING IS NOT NECESSARY AT ALL.

This may be a little controversial and annoying, frustrating even, if you are suffering right now while you read these words. I'm not writing it to annoy or anger you though. I'm writing it, because it's the truth and I know this from many years of direct experience.

This understanding had a great impact on me. Just as big an impact as learning that peace or pain is a choice. To recognise suffering only takes place when you are resisting, was to me, hugely empowering.

This is because it means I can learn to not resist and cultivate an entirely different mode of operation. A mode of operation where I am present and master of my experience, rather than a victim of circumstance.

It's still a work in progress for me, but once I understood the rules of the game, I started to enjoy playing it again. Like when I was a little girl, carefree and happy, full of the joys of life.

You too can gain a clearer understanding of what pain really is. Not just by reading about my experience and understanding of pain, but also by adopting the same playful approach and starting to pay attention to your own body's signals.

In my experience, you are unlikely to be able to do this without an effective meditation technique. This is because you will be so immersed in your current experience, you will not be able to see beyond it. Plus, even when you can see there is a choice, it is still necessary to have a tool. A tool which will take you to peace automatically, at the same time as systematically releasing all stored stress. The most effective techniques I have ever come across, are The Bright Path Ishayas' Ascension Attitudes.

Not only is the practice of Ascension very fast and effective, but the ongoing support and guidance you receive is an incredibly important part of changing your relationship with thoughts, emotions, and body sensations. It's so much easier and more effective to do this as part of a community, than it is to do it by yourself.

I'll talk more about this in part three.

Chapter 11
The mind-body connection

To understand pain, it is important to understand the relationship between the mind and the body.

Basically, every thought we believe to be true is felt by the body. A belief is just a thought that is held in the unconscious mind. Put another way, if we believe it to be true, the thought runs continually on a loop in our unconscious mind.

This requires a lot of energy to sustain and we are not even aware this is what we are doing. We are not conscious this process is happening. It is running on a loop automatically.

It's no wonder we get tired and overwhelmed when we are continually playing thoughts on repeat.

I was shocked when I realised this was what was happening in my mind. Not because someone told me it was true, but because I got to see it for myself, as I became more proficient at witnessing the mechanism of the mind.

Thinking can be compared to a giant iceberg. The thoughts and thinking we are consciously aware of, are like the tip of the iceberg which sticks out of the water; a small fraction of what is going on beneath the surface. The majority of thinking is like the larger part of the thought iceberg and it takes place below the surface in the unconscious mind.

This is why it is so difficult to change our minds about anything. We don't have conscious access to the thought patterns which are playing on repeat because they are hidden beneath the surface.

This continual unconscious thinking has a great impact on our body because of the mind / body connection.

Let me illustrate this for you by doing a short exercise.

Imagine for a moment that I am cutting up a lemon and I hand you a segment. You bite into it and the lemon juice squeezes into your mouth. What happens? Do you notice that your saliva glands activate and you react to the idea of a lemon, as if you were actually biting into it? The thought causes a reaction in the body and the impact is felt immediately.

Let me give you some more examples of when the mind/body connection is evident. If you are angry your jaw can tighten, your fist can tense up and you can also sometimes experience a tightening across your chest. If you are anxious you will feel this in your stomach. Like the saying 'sick to the stomach' or 'I have butterflies', is a sign of anxiety or nervousness. If you are embarrassed or self-conscious about something, your cheeks may tinge red as the blood flows to the surface.

So, you can see every thought we have literally has an impact on our body. Our bodies are affected by thinking and feeling.

We can see this in other people too. There is a whole science behind the mind/body connection. Many people research and learn about body language and how to read another person by their posture and facial expression.

The obvious one I remember hearing about when I was at school was, if your cross your arms you are feeling defensive. You may want to hide something or feel the need to protect yourself from what is being said to you. It could also be that you perceive something is expected of you, something you are not comfortable with, or don't want to do.

We like to hide what we are thinking from the world because we have learnt there is something wrong with us. Therefore, we obviously don't want anyone else to know what we are thinking or feeling.

The trouble is, it is not something we can hide. Our bodies respond to our thoughts, enabling us to be read like an open book for those who understand the signals.

I always used to hate this idea and tried to mask the signals, so people couldn't tell what I was thinking or feeling.

I needn't have worried, because I have also learnt since then, even though other people think they can mind read, they are usually not accurate. This is because we have so many thoughts flowing through our minds every day, so the messages are often not clear. However, we all do an unconscious process of interpretation and come to conclusions about what another person thinks and feels about us.

This leads to a lot of confusion and misunderstanding between people when they communicate with each other. Everyone thinks they know what the other person is saying and reacts based on that interpretation. We don't bother to ask the relevant questions, which are pertinent to the interaction, to uncover the true intention of the person we are communicating with.

The more stressed you are, the less clearly you can see, or hear the intention of another person. We see and hear what we think we are seeing and hearing. Our beliefs colour the way we see and hear, so we jump to conclusions all the time and react with anger or get upset by what we perceive is being said or done to us.

As my stress levels reduced, I became more aware of this misunderstanding in my communication. My clarity in perception has become clearer and clearer. This makes it easier and therefore less stressful to communicate with others. It also means I can ask the pertinent questions, which uncover the conclusions drawn by others from what I have said to them.

I am able to remain calm while I communicate, not in a contrived way, as I tried and failed to do in the past. But in a stable and sustainable way. When I am calm, I am able to discern the real meaning behind what people are saying to me. I am also able to recognise when people are taking what I say in the wrong way, so I can clarify what I mean and put it another way. This enables the other person to realise the true meaning of my words and the real intention behind them.

Without this clarity I used to jump to conclusions all the time and this had a knock-on effect on my body. I perceived a lot of people as rude, inconsiderate, and thoughtless. When really, they were just very stressed, fearful, and not seeing clearly, so their words and actions were reflecting this.

My body took the toll of these incorrectly perceived interactions. I spent more and more time by myself, as the tension built up to unbearable levels. Alone time was the only time I could relax and be myself.

It is quite incredible how much tension can be stored in the body. Unless you release some of this stored tension, the body will start to malfunction and snap under the pressure, leading to all sorts of painful and debilitating health conditions.

The only time you truly rest, is when the mind is at rest.

As long as we are thinking, which is essentially activity in the mind, there will be activity in the body which prevents the body from its natural activity of maintaining health and normal body functioning.

In order to allow the mind to rest, we must interrupt the habitual pattern of thinking all the time, so the body can rest and take over its healing and maintenance process.

Let's take a closer look at what happens when the mental, emotional and physical cycle runs amok.

Chapter 12
Mental, emotional, physical

I read somewhere, quite some time ago, that emotions are just a record of the past.

I found this concept intriguing and worth investigating to see if it matched my experience.

After some investigation, I am inclined to agree with this idea. The reasons I came to this conclusion are: Firstly, when I am fully present, there does not appear to be any emotion flowing through me; Secondly, I notice there is usually a story from the past which goes with the emotional feeling; And thirdly, emotion only intensifies when I resist it, and resistance is a previously learnt habit.

Let me expand on these reasons. Firstly, being present is a very enlivened state of being. When I experience this state, I don't notice any emotion. There is no commentary about what is happening, what has happened, or what may happen in the future. My attention is only on what is in front of me right now.

I may leave this state of being present, which I usually recognise by an uncomfortable feeling, or an ache, body sensation or symptom of some kind. Less often I recognise I am thinking so when I notice any of these, I use my technique to become present once again. Sometimes I catch it quite soon and it's a subtle experience and sometimes it has to get more intense before it captures my attention. But for me it is always a sign I am no longer present.

Even when I do experience an emotion, which is in direct response to something which is happening to me right now, there is always internal dialogue that relates back to the past. It is never about what is happening now. It is because of something which happened to me before, (that I have not let go of), which effects my experience in THIS moment. I therefore deduce it is a record of the past that is being set free and I needn't analyse it or find a reason for it. Nor do I need to battle with what is happening which caused the emotion to bubble up. Analysing or fighting it would cause more thinking and therefore more tension/potential illness in the body.

It is easier not to argue with people about what is happening now. I simply choose to pay attention and let the answer come to me, or let the emotional response fade away. The speed of which it fades away is closely related to how surrendered I am.

For example, if I allow it 30%, it is easier but still quite uncomfortable. If I allow it 60%, then it is a lot less intense and therefore much easier to manage the feeling passing through me. However, if I allow the emotion 100%, it is gone in a split second and does not return.

The second reason (I notice there is usually a story from the past which goes with the emotional feeling) is something I have identified from paying attention when the emotion is intense. I have seen this evidence many times and came to the realisation the dialogue is formed into a story.

The story is one I have seen myself thinking over and over like a broken record. It loops in my mind, only stopping when I notice and choose to stop thinking.

If you don't stop thinking, you recreate the emotion again and again until you get fed up and distract yourself with something to mask the feeling. For example, food, drugs, alcohol, sleep, Netflix, social media, or online gaming etc.

The stories we play in our minds are of no use to us at all. They keep us from being present, recreate the associated feelings and get in the way of living our lives.

The third reason (emotion only intensifies when I resist it and resistance is a learnt habit) is something I recognised after learning resistance is the cause of all suffering.

It took a little while to recognise this for myself, because I couldn't actually identify all the ways I had learnt to resist. I read somewhere, I forget where, you resist by repressing, suppressing, and expressing emotions. I began to recognise that this is true and then started to explore this theory and identified when I was doing any of these three ways of resisting. I discovered I did this with emotions, with what is happening right now and by trying to think my way out of how I was feeling.

The biggest eye opener for me regarding resistance was, if you express the emotion you could be resisting it. I did not understand, or even agree with this when I first read about resistance.

The difference between repression and suppression, for the sake of clarity, is helpful to understand. Repression is when you <u>unconsciously</u> push down your feelings and natural impulses. Whereas, suppression is when you <u>consciously</u> push down your feelings and impulses.

Often, we only recognise it when we are suppressing something, because it is a conscious process we are aware of.

Repression happens as an unconscious process, so we can be doing it and have no idea we are repressing something. This of course makes it a bit tricky to see whether you are resisting something, or not.

I have now become aware of the majority of the ways I unconsciously resist my experience. One thing is very clear to me, if I'm resisting anything, my experience becomes uncomfortable or intense. If I continue to resist, it builds up in intensity becoming painful and unbearable.

Any symptoms I have in any given moment become more uncomfortable and intense when I am resisting them. It becomes easier and easier to recognise when I am resisting, because my body tells me. It gets louder and more intense, until I notice and take action to change my state and allow the flow of emotion through my body.

Emotion is just energy in motion e-motion. The body is healthy and functional when the flow of energy is unhindered. When we resist, we stop the natural flow which enlivens us and allows homeostasis to take place. Homeostasis is the body's way of rebalancing, keeping itself fully functional and in good working order.

This is why resistance causes symptoms and pain to intensify. The flow of energy gets blocked and backs up with nowhere to go, which means it stays in that part of the body and stagnates becoming more dense, causing problems in that area.

It also takes a lot of energy to continue to resist the body's natural process of homeostasis, which causes fatigue. This resisting pattern then causes tension in that area of the body, which does not ease, until you recognise there is tension and do something about it.

Doing something about it may look like having a warm bath, a massage, or resting on the sofa etc. These are all great ways to relax and unwind, but they do not resolve the cause of the tension.

Until we learn to let emotion flow through us unhindered, we will continue to store tension, block homeostasis, and create more pain and suffering.

This brings me to the expression of emotions, like when we cry, shout and scream. Now, I always used to think when I had a good cry and then felt better afterwards that I was releasing some stress from my system. But after reading this was not the case, even though I didn't agree, I thought I had better check it out in case it was true, and I was missing a trick.

After some experimentation with this, I discovered there were definitely times when I would cry and yet I was not fully letting go. In my experience, I was building up intensity until it was unbearable, and tears would start flowing. In reality, I had just released the excess stress, but the underlying pattern remained the same. I did feel better, however, that feeling did not last long.

It was the same with anger. Not much triggers me these days, unless some deeply held emotion finds its way to the surface in response to my daily meditation practice. Then I do become more easily triggered and more reactive to the people and world around me. It was a while before I got to see what was really happening. But eventually I discovered that by venting, in the form of shouting, I was actually still resisting the flow of energy within me.

I didn't feel any better by shouting, in fact I came to realise shouting meant I pushed it back down again and created more anger and more angry words.

As I became more and more alert and attentive to when my voice raised even a tiny bit, I became aware I was not necessarily saying exactly what I wanted to say. I was often trying to express myself in a way that did not upset the other person, or I edited my words to be more palatable to the other person. Often, I did this because I was afraid of what their response might be if I said what I really wanted to say.

I had been doing this for so many years, it was difficult to discern initially what I actually wanted to say. But with practise and just going for it, I got better and better at not editing my words and saying what I needed to say immediately. Saying something the moment it occurs to you, actually makes your words clearer.

This is because your words are not charged with the repressed energy which builds up when you hold back what naturally wants to come forth.

When you no longer edit your words, they have a greater impact on others. They hear your intent, rather than their interpreted version of your words. They also, in my experience, tend to take you more seriously and respond more kindly to what you say.

It is like someone clears a path for your words to go directly into a person's conscious awareness and the words no longer get lost in translation.

It makes communication a lot easier and you don't build up stress from all the unsaid words and associated emotion which seem to be stored inside you.

I also find my mind is quieter when I say what I need to in the moment. I no longer need to practise what I want to say. I have come to trust the right, or most appropriate words will just flow from me in any given situation.

There was one occasion when I just spoke without editing which totally surprised me. My mum was telling me to do something I didn't want to do. I said, "It is my choice not yours". To which she replied, "Yes you are right, it is your choice". This was not the response I expected! I had thought she would be angry with me, when in fact she responded exactly as I would have liked her to respond.

It's curious how what we think is 'a nice way of putting things', can in fact be inflammatory, and speaking ruthlessly can be perceived as more gentle!

Emotions can definitely cloud your experience and lead to miscommunication. As I have released most of the stored emotional backlog in me, I have found I can see things much more clearly than before.

I can now see how a person is upset from their own situation and it's not actually about me. I have noticed I can see the upset and not feel it. I can be compassionate and caring whilst still considering my own needs. This stops me from reacting to their state and allows me to remain calm and collected, even in the face of extreme anger or sadness. This puts me in a much better position to be able to help them.

These are some of the discoveries I've made on the emotional side of the experience. However, the picture is not complete unless we also talk about the mental and physical aspects of the human experience. Plus, look at how they are all connected.

. . .

The mental part of us is about our mind and how we use it.

For a start, what is the mind? When you start to meditate, you get to witness the mechanism of the mind and observe how it functions. As I stopped thinking all the time, I started to recognise the mind is not what I first believed it to be.

The mind in reality is just a bunch of thoughts hanging out together. They hang out in the unconscious part of us, so we don't necessarily see them. One thought held in the unconscious mind is enough to attract other thoughts and before you know it, you have more than you can handle. These thoughts have become an entity unto themselves which we usually refer to as 'the ego'.

The ego is just an idea or opinion we have about ourselves.

That's it.

For the first seven years of our lives we are like sponges, soaking up everything we see and hear. We have no discernment of whether it is useful, or true. If we heard or saw something again and again, it becomes stored as a belief. True, simply because it was what we experienced repetitively and therefore becomes lodged in our unconscious as a truth.

A belief is just a thought we hold in the mind.

We learnt these beliefs from our parents, our teachers, other adults, and our peers. We can have beliefs which are in direct opposition to each other. We can believe we are not good enough simply because we were told it again and again, overtly, or covertly.

The mind stores anything that we conclude is true. We often have no proof of this, other than somebody told us a long time ago. But once we decide it is true, it's stored until proven otherwise.

In order to hold these beliefs in the mind, the belief/thought continually plays in the mind, over and over again. It requires a lot of energy to continually think something and it has a continual detrimental effect on us, as every belief impacts on every cell in our entire body.

It's no wonder we are tired.

The belief system / ego mind is like the puppet master. Every time thinking happens, our body receives the order and has no choice but to follow the command.

. . .

The body is like the dumping ground for the mind.

It is the obedient child which tries to follow every command, but with the mixed messages and continual flood of information, it isn't always easy. So the loudest and most frequent command is the one which has the biggest impact.

What is the most frequent dialogue in your head right now?

Is it positive or negative?

Is it coherent or jumbled?

Does it make you feel good or bad?

Whatever the content of the dialogue running through your head every day is, puts an extreme amount of pressure on your body. And the stress just piles up and up. Eventually this takes a toll on your nervous system and the body starts to struggle and fail in some parts.

Unless we release some of this stored stress, we will get sick and suffer from a whole variety of health issues.

I recognise, by the state of my body, how significant an impact my thoughts and emotions have had on it over the years. I didn't even realise this, until enough stress was released from my nervous system. As I continued to use the Ascension techniques, my body started to uncurl and rebalance.

Another thing I noticed, was how different my face looked after a 10-day retreat I attended in 2012. I was brushing my teeth on the last morning and I suddenly caught a glimpse of my reflection in the mirror. I paused and looked more closely and to my delight I looked about 10 years younger. The lines around my eyes had softened and my whole face looked lighter, fresher somehow and the haggard look had disappeared.

The next time I noticed a significant difference was after my 'Mastery of the Self' retreat later on the same year. It sounds daft really, but I noticed my ears were floppy and flexible and no longer sore to touch. I hadn't even realised they could be like this. They had been rigid and inflexible for so long, I just thought that's what they were supposed to be like.

I got confirmation of this not long after that, from a reflexology practitioner, when I visited her to receive a treatment. She commented on how flexible and pliable my feet were and how healthy and relaxed I was, compared to when I had last seen her six months earlier.

It was a great surprise to her; she had never seen such a dramatic and fast improvement before. This led to her booking on a course with me to learn the Ascension techniques, so she could benefit as well.

Since that time, I have continued to periodically notice changes in my face and body as I continue to teach and use these remarkable techniques. Many parts of my body, which had previously felt tense and solid, have softened, relaxed, and become more flexible. I have also experienced improvement in my vision and asthma symptoms.

My eyes are the most unexpected part of me to change. I had, years before, started doing eye exercises to improve my vision, following a series of headaches that were getting worse and worse. But this was spontaneous and gradual improvement which surprised me, because it required no effort and just happened by itself after each closed eye Ascension session.

I started using the Ascension techniques eyes open, to see if that would also have an impact on my vision. I noticed I held a lot of tension in and around my eyes. No wonder they didn't work properly! We just call it short-sightedness, wear glasses and think no more of it. But in my experience and after quite extensive research, I discovered that eyes are governed by the mind. This is because the eyes take in so much input from the world around us that we need the mind to organise it and make coherent sense of this data, so we can recognise what we are seeing.

I find this fascinating and the inquisitive part of my nature likes to push the boundaries and explore all the possibilities of what this discovery can provide.

This is a work in progress, I still need glasses to see. However, my prescription is reduced, and I can sometimes see completely clearly without my glasses on.

It's one of the ways I recognise I am no longer present. My eyes feel sore and strained; therefore, I don't see as well. I take it as a cue to close my eyes and use the Ascension techniques.

With my asthma, I have found it has gradually become easier to breathe and I no longer need to use my inhaler as often as I used to. Plus, when I do need to use it, the symptoms are only mild compared to how they used to be several years ago. I no longer experience any full-blown asthma attacks, just a shortness of breath which slows me down a bit.

There is no timetable for improvement of health conditions and no promises that can ever be made about how fast or completely your body will heal. However, allowing the mind to rest, so the body can fully rest, initiates a deep healing process to begin. This has been a much more efficient and effective way to heal my body than anything else I have discovered.

Chapter 13
Fight or flight

The fight or flight reaction is one that affects us all. Most of us live in this mode of operation for quite a large part of our daily life.

It is very destructive to our long-term health to remain in fight or flight mode, so it's important to understand what it is and recognise when it is activated within us.

The fight or flight response is a very useful and necessary bodily response that activates in order to keep us safe and out of harm's way.

It is important to recognise the role of emotions in our lives so we can begin to allow them to help guide us in our daily lives.

Many of us prefer to focus on logic and rationalisation, rather than our emotions. But emotions have a purpose. Emotions like fear or anger are vital messengers. They are basically signals that help us to meet our need for self preservation and safety.

It could be dangerous for us to be indecisive if we are presented with a threat to our survival, so the brain receives information from our senses through the most primitive, reactive part of our brain first. Then, this part of the brain communicates with the rest of our brain and our body, to create signals we can't ignore - powerful emotions and symptoms.

The fight or flight response is a physiological response which is triggered when we feel a strong emotion like fear or anger. Fear is the emotion we experience in response to danger or a threat. Anxiety is closely related to fear and a common emotion many people now experience on a daily basis.

The fight or flight response evolved to enable us to react quickly when presented with a potentially dangerous situation. It is a normal and very useful response, which activates our body to run away, stand and fight, or sometimes to freeze so we can become a less visible target.

In order to achieve these fast reactions, the fight or flight response uses all the bodies resources and redirects them to the limbs and brain to enable us to run away or defend ourselves.

This means the major organs and usual functions, like digestion and the immune system, power down to reduce activity to a very low level that keeps us alive, but no more.

It is an important and normal response which serves a purpose. However, in our modern-day world where there are no sabre tooth tigers to attack us, it can often be triggered far too often.

A good analogy is the smoke alarm. A smoke alarm is designed to alert us to the danger of smoke and fire, but it cannot distinguish the difference between burnt food and a house fire. The first is not a threat, whilst the second is potentially fatal, yet the response of the alarm is the same.

Most of life is no longer about fighting or escaping predators. These days the fight or flight mode is much more likely to be triggered by internal threats. For example, worries about a job interview, exam, or a social situation we find daunting. Or perhaps anger because of an interaction, communication or situation that seems unfair, rude, or unacceptable to us.

When we feel anxious, fearful, or angry the fight or flight response is initiated in our body. We then experience a range of physical symptoms which temporarily change the way the body is functioning, to enable a rapid response to the perceived threat.

Some areas of the body will increase in activity, whilst other areas will decrease in activity and functioning.

Increased activity:

Heart beats quicker and harder - coronary arteries dilate and blood pressure rises.

Circulation increases blood supply and oxygen to the brain, muscles and limbs. Muscles tense for action.

Brain activity changes - we think less and react more instinctively.

Lungs take in more oxygen and release more carbon dioxide.

Liver releases extra sugar for energy.

Sweating increases to speed heat loss.

Adrenal glands release adrenalin to fuel response.

Decreased activity:

Digestion slows down, stomach and small intestines reduce activity.

Mouth goes dry from the constriction of blood vessels in salivary glands.

Kidney, large intestine and bladder slow down.

Immune response decreases.

It is helpful to know what the physiological responses are, so we can address them without it leading to a perpetual reactive cycle. It's so easy to get caught in a never-ending loop.

We think there is something wrong and that leads to an anxious feeling, which in turn leads to physical symptoms, such as a dry mouth, hyperventilation and / or tension in the stomach.

The reactive cycle looks something like this:

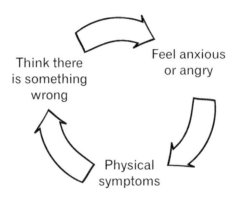

Think there
is something
wrong

Feel anxious
or angry

Physical
symptoms

It is normal for the brain to register pain or discomfort, because these are vital indicators of threat and danger. The physiological changes can be very uncomfortable, or painful and can lead to us concluding something is wrong.

Which there may be. But the mind can and probably will continuously search for reasons, or worry about the situation getting worse, or it never-ending. This can keep the cycle going with symptoms increasing each time the cycle repeats.

The fight or flight response can cause a whole host of problems and dysfunction in the body, especially when there is no outlet to utilise the physiological responses.

It all gets pent up inside us causing the body to malfunction, building up levels of adrenaline and stress. Tension is created and stored which means the body becomes more and more rigid over time.

This is not a healthy, or enjoyable way to function in the world and it doesn't have to be this way.

The fight or flight mechanism is useful when we are in danger, but it needn't be activated for so much of the time in everyday life.

Our natural state is rest and relax mode, which is easy to access and effortless to maintain. In rest and relax mode we can respond in a more conscious way, act how we choose to act in response to current circumstances. Our body is able to operate efficiently and can therefore maintain equilibrium with ease. Healthy cells are automatically created and maintained. Healing is swift and effective.

This natural state of rest and relax can be easily sustained when the mind is calm and still. An optimal state of health becomes much more readily available.

Chapter 14
What is stress?

Stress is something pretty much everyone experiences to some degree or another. We know we get stressed and we can give some examples of what causes us to be stressed, but we don't necessarily know exactly what stress is and how we create it in the first place.

Feeling stressed is something which happens when our nervous system is overloaded.

So how does our nervous system get overloaded?

We take on stress every day, both emotional stress and physical stress.

Emotional stress is accumulated by situations we perceive to be difficult, annoying, confusing, or scary. Once you start taking on stress emotionally, it starts to snowball, because the more stress you accumulate, the more things stress you out.

Let me give you some examples of emotional stressors. For example, if you have an argument with somebody, or someone is being controlling towards you, telling you what to do all the time. Stress could also be created because there is something you want, or need to do, like giving a speech and you aren't confident about doing it. Or you're at an event, it could be anything from a wedding, a funeral or a social gathering and it's noisy with a lot of activity going on all around you. Too much information at once will overload your nervous system and you will start to take on stress.

You will notice by the examples I gave; it isn't just negative situations or interactions which cause you to take on stress. At a funeral it's obvious you will feel emotional and take on stress.

But equally at a wedding, which is an enjoyable event, you will also likely take on stress. Although a wedding is enjoyable, it is also noisy, emotional, and continuously stimulating.

My kids used to enjoy making me jump by leaping out from behind a corner. They thought it was hilarious when I gasped and jumped in surprise. I enjoyed it too, but I would have taken on stress each time due to the adrenaline pumping round my body!

There are also physical stressors. For example: eating too much or the wrong type of food, drugs - prescribed and recreational, alcohol, physical injuries, pollution, and the list goes on...

Stress is simply an overload on the nervous system and many situations, environments and communities will create an overload. Sometimes they are horrible and sometimes enjoyable. Either way it puts stress on the nervous system.

We all have busy lives these days, where a lot of activity happens day in and day out. We often don't get a chance to stop and pause for a moment and catch our breath.

There are also a lot of people, you may be one of them, who don't get a restful sleep at night. Sleep is the main way we rest and release the stresses from the day before. But, if we're not getting enough sleep, are restless or wake up in the night and can't get back to sleep, we are not releasing enough stress.

This means we need to find another way to rest and release stress.

The only way we get complete rest, is when the mind is still too. Because of the mind-body connection, (which was covered in a previous chapter), when there is activity in the mind, there is activity in the body and vice versa.

So even when we are chilling out on a sofa, if we are watching television, or thinking about something, we will not be resting our body completely. This is because the activity in the mind, creates activity in the body. It might feel relaxing, but we are not experiencing enough rest to throw off the stored stress. We may even take on more stress in that moment if there is a high level of stimuli.

If you are thinking about an argument with a friend or family member, then you will likely be taking on more stress, even though you are sitting down with your feet up, supposedly resting.

The key, therefore, is finding a way to still the mind. Or rather finding a technique which brings you to a direct experience of stillness and silence. Then the mind naturally follows suit and stills, without any effort on your part.

Chapter 15
Habitual patterns

We so often think we are failing or not doing well enough in our lives. This is not only untrue, it is also just an habitual way of thinking.

Habits are useful to us; they are a natural part of us, and we need them to operate efficiently.

For example, when we learn a new skill like driving a car, we are not very coordinated. There is a lot to learn and do all at the same time and it takes us a while to get the hang of it. With repetition and practise we get more proficient at the new skill and it becomes a habit.

Once it becomes a habit, it frees us up to do extra tasks, or carry out the skill more easily and quickly. With the car example, it means we can then drive safely and turn up the radio, or have a conversation with our passenger at the same time.

So, it's very useful to create habits in many ways.

The only problem is, some of the habits we cultivate are unhelpful, or no longer helpful to us. For example, if we were told over and over we aren't very good at something, or we're told we are stupid or ugly, eventually it will be laid down in our unconscious mind. It will become a filter for everything we try to do in the future and every situation we find ourselves in.

This type of habit is therefore limiting and often debilitating. These types of habitual thinking patterns in the mind will stop us from doing what we would like to do, or will cause us to perceive something as a threat.

The filter of an habitual thought pattern, say for example 'I'm not good enough', will often mean we don't hear the true message. So, when somebody tells us they are upset with us for some reason or other, we could perceive their words as a criticism of us and become defensive, argumentative, or even hostile.

Once something is laid down as a habit, it is really difficult to change, because it is in our unconscious mind and therefore inaccessible to us.

It's the same with physical pain. For a start, the habitual thought patterns are affecting the body, so that it is not work efficiently or effectively. But also, once we start to have pain, the pathways in the brain get used to the signals and it becomes a pattern of thinking, and therefore creates a pattern of response in the body.

I have been shocked at how used to pain I became. To the point I no longer had any idea of what it could be like to be free of pain.

I also discovered I became used to being on high alert with my body. Every twinge, every ache, every tension was noticed, and a dialogue would start up about it. Why was it there; what caused it; how I could make it better; what if it means something is seriously wrong; what if it never heals etc.

This habit of noticing my body, meant I was almost constantly paying attention to every symptom, and it was exhausting.

The only way to change any habit which clearly no longer serves you and is detrimental to your health, is to use the system by which you created the habit in the first place.

Repetition and persistence.

Only this time you will do it consciously, rather than unconsciously, to cultivate habits which are useful and beneficial to you.

The best and most effective way I know to change habits, is to meditate.

And I don't mean follow a guided meditation, or a meditation that just relaxes you. Both are useful and beneficial. But they don't change your relationship with your mind, or your body.

No, I mean finding and using a technique that will mechanically take your attention within, to a direct experience of stillness, silence, and space.

Not only is it very restful to use a technique like this, it is also very effective at cultivating a new habit and allowing the old limiting habits to dissolve.

I will talk more in Part Three about the Ascension techniques I use and have found most effective for cultivating a new habit and changing my experience quickly with no effort whatsoever. These techniques easily and gently retrain the brain to function more coherently and fluidly. Thus, making life easier, calmer, more alive and enjoyable again.

Chapter 16
Self-preservation

Safety and feeling safe is an important topic which doesn't often get discussed. Most of us have a comprehensive defence mechanism in place to keep us safe. Self-preservation tactics can, however, be very harmful to our bodies: holding in excess tension, heightening emotional responses, and causing us to see danger, when there isn't any.

When we unconsciously perceive a situation as hostile, or threatening, we activate the flight or fight response, which as I said in a previous chapter has a detrimental impact on the body.

So, it's important to begin to recognise you have a defence mechanism and learn how to identify when it activates within you.

In the last chapter we talked about habits, how and why they are formed. One of the main reasons we develop a defence mechanism habit, is to ensure our safety in all situations.

Our defence mechanism is personal to us, based on past events and interactions. Some of us have a defence mechanism that is based on lies and situations which ceased to happen a long time ago and are therefore null and void.

Our unconscious mind does not know it is no longer relevant though. It still activates at the tiniest of perceived threats and confuses and complicates every interaction. It will also cause us distress, prior to certain events, in preparation for danger.

It's good to be careful and aware of anything which can cause you actual bodily harm, of course. But a lot of the perceived threats aren't real and are simply a reaction to something someone says to you which triggers fear, or anger. This can then label this person as a threat and you may react by shouting or leaving the situation in a hurry.

Later on, when you are in an environment in which you feel safe, you may regret your words and even be confused as to why you left the situation.

It will likely cause a dialogue to start up in your mind. Going over and over the situation, to work out what happened and how you can prevent it from happening again.

You may even hold on to your anger, or fear and be hostile or fearful the next time you see this person. In which case, you are unlikely to hear what they are saying, without the past interaction colouring this new interaction.

Over time this builds up into a more and more intense reaction and the emotional response will feel increasingly uncomfortable. It can lead to rage or an inability to be around other people without feeling anxious, fearful, or overwhelmed. It can also be masked as irritation, or annoyance.

This will also have a knock-on effect on your body and your level of tension will rise and your health can suffer. Which in turn can lead to pain and dysfunction in various parts of the body.

I had a very strong defence mechanism which was triggered every day by anything and everything. The level of tension in my body was extreme and caused me a lot of pain, in a lot of places. It also caused my spine to become distorted and my breathing to worsen. I experienced frequent headaches, had a perpetual sore throat, or blocked up nose. My jaw ached all the time and my neck and shoulders were always painful.

And that was before I was diagnosed with M.E. and then later Symphysis Pubis Dysfunction. These two conditions were so debilitating, that I was bed ridden for quite some time.

Learning how my defence mechanism operated made my life much easier. It enabled me to relax and feel more safe and secure in situations which had previously created a high level of anxiety in me.

The main way I discovered my defence mechanism, was by simply becoming more aware. Day by day, week by week, I started to see where I held tension in my body and I also got to see the thoughts which were creating the anxious feelings.

The great thing about the Ascension practice I use, is that it is mechanical. I didn't need to work anything out, or change anything about myself. The Ascension techniques did the job for me. All I had to do was close my eyes 2 or 3 times a day for 20 minutes. The patterns within my mind started to dissolve and the emotional responses automatically calmed down.

I could also use the Ascension techniques with my eyes open as I went about my day too. When I noticed something trigger me and activate anxious, or angry thoughts and feelings, I was able to become present and calm again.

It was a gradual retraining process and was uncomfortable at times. I realised the only way I was going to feel better in the long run, was to allow my emotional responses. Emotions that I had been pushing down for decades and did not want to revisit, so the intensity was high, and it was difficult to allow them.

What I learnt over time, was the resistance created a higher level of intensity and so I became more motivated to allow. Then the emotional feeling became much more soft and gentle.

As I continued using the techniques, I developed a stronger sense of peace which was palpable and stable. Along with this new peaceful and happy state, was a body which became much less tense and more flexible. Plus, the pain levels decreased dramatically, and my health improved.

Self-preservation can be detrimental to your health. Discovering this for yourself, will free your body from the constraints of the 'puppet mastermind' and you will be able to live life in a more natural and relaxed manner.

The world has dangers in it, yes. But not as many as the mind will lead you to believe. Discerning whether there is actual danger, instead of a fictitious danger, can make a big difference to the state of your mind and also to the physical state of your body. This will mean you are actually more able to act quickly and effectively if there is real danger.

We don't need such a comprehensive defence mechanism in place as we can live safely without a defence mechanism at all.

Presence is far more reliable and effective at keeping you safe.

Chapter 17
Awareness

Awareness is everything when it comes to pain. We cannot make any changes if we are not aware of what is causing the pain in the first place.

So often we are given medication to reduce or get rid of the pain we are experiencing. This may make life more bearable in the short term. But long term it dulls our senses and interrupts our natural mind-body connection, masking our ability to discover the true cause of our suffering.

I consider myself very lucky I could not tolerate Morphine. I was given Morphine many years ago, when other pain medication did not even come close to reducing the level of pain I was in. This was at that time immediately after childbirth, when my Symphysis Pubis Dysfunction did not resolve, as it supposedly should have done.

The first time I took Morphine, the pain reduced dramatically, and I experienced relief. The next dose the following day rendered me incapable of moving off the bed, dizzy, disorientated and with little pain reduction. So I stopped taking it there and then.

I say I feel lucky, because I witnessed my father, (who did experience some relief from taking Morphine) gradually progress onto stronger and stronger doses to achieve the same effect. In time it appeared to do very little for the pain, but he insisted on needing it, as he was convinced it gave him some relief.

Pain medication is a tricky one. We don't want to experience the pain, so we will do almost anything to make it go away. But in truth, the medication to reduce pain, can in fact cause pain. I'm not saying it's wrong to take pain medication. It is an individual choice dependent on your own personal situation. Using pain medication, can be like putting a band aid on an open festering wound and expecting it to heal. It may reduce the pain for a while, but it does not address the root cause of the pain and so in time the physical condition can (and often does) get worse.

Awareness is therefore a crucial thing to consciously develop, so we can discover the underlying causes, as well as learn how to understand the mechanism of pain and how it is operating. This enables you to do things differently, so you can get different results.

We have learnt to put our awareness, our attention, on the physical world only. We focus on the physical body sensations, the thoughts about our body sensations and the emotional reaction to the thoughts about our body sensations.

In doing this, we have reduced or limited our experience of ourselves and the world around us.

It's not wrong, but it does mean we only have part of the picture. We don't see the whole picture, so we come to conclusions about the state of our body which are inaccurate or incomplete.

In order to have a greater, or fuller understanding of our physical body, we need to put everything into context.

For this we need awareness. And it is so easy to do. All we need to do is pay attention. Be attentive to our body and world around us, and the answers are revealed to us.

This is where the mind is a hindrance. When we think we know what is going on and have all the answers, we often miss the bigger picture. We miss the one piece of information which could completely change our perception and experience of our body right now. When the mind is active, it captures most of our attention, so we can't see what is going on right in front of us.

One useful ingredient for expanding your conscious awareness of your body and world is to be curious.

Curiosity is a very useful tool in exploring the situation, or state you find yourself in. When the pain is intense and there is no sign it will abate any time soon, you can become curious about the pain. Bring your attention to that part of your body which is in pain and simply observe it.

In doing this you will become more present and, more importantly, the dialogue about your pain will cease. When the dialogue ceases, your perception of the symptoms start to change.

This is because the dialogue is providing a continual stream of instructions to your body. These instructions create a response in the body, and this prevents or interferes with your body's natural healing process.

Expanding your awareness, also provides space for answers to be recognised in your mind. For example, it may be as simple as 'Sit down and put your feet up' or 'have a drink of water', or simply 'breathe'. Your body needs rest, it needs water and it needs air, along with a whole host of other options that will assist it in the healing process.

Awareness gives us the ability to discern when we need to do something, or when our body simply needs some rest.

This beautiful quote from Garuda, a fellow Bright Path Ishaya teacher, sums up the potential power in awareness:

"There is nothing that can withstand the power and light of awareness. Awareness is the light that sets us free. To shine awareness on our judgements, dissolves them. And when the boundaries are removed, by nothing more than 'seeing with awareness', the mind is not bound by anything. It is our judgements that keep the mind limited and it is awareness that sets it free."

When the mind is free, the body is free. Free to do its job of self-replicating and running itself like a well-oiled machine.

Awareness keeps it well lubricated and running efficiently and effectively.

When talking about awareness, I like to use this analogy: Awareness is like turning on the light in a darkened room. When it's dark in a room we cannot manoeuvre around the room very easily, we bump into things and trip over them because we can't see them. We can't find objects we're looking for because we can't locate them. Also, objects look very different in reduced light, we might think a coat hanging on a chair is an intruder who has come to hurt us. We can't see what is really there because there is not enough light to see clearly.

It's the same with awareness. We can only see all the information and all the pertinent ways of helping us to be healthy and whole if we turn up the light of awareness. We need to stop thinking for a moment and just pay attention. To observe and listen to our body's signals, so we can do what needs to be done to heal and reduce pain.

In paying attention, I often notice my body is tense in a certain area and by observing this tension, without commentary from the mind, the body naturally rebalances and adjusts itself. Healing happens without us needing to do anything at all.

As if by magic. But it's not magic, it's biology. Homeostasis. All we need to do is get out of the way and let the body get on with its job and heal itself.

It's easy to cultivate awareness. But we do need a tool to help us shift our attention from the content of thought, emotion, and body sensations to the context of stillness, silence, and space.

Chapter 18
Content / Context

It can be very useful to learn about the difference between content and context. When we put our attention only on content, we live a very limited life full of pain and suffering.

What I mean by content and context is simply where you put your attention. I didn't realise when this concept was first presented to me, that there was anything other than content. I didn't think of it as content of course, because that was all there was in my experience. It was just my life and what I was aware of within my environment.

Content is everything we can see, hear, touch, taste, and smell. This includes thoughts, feelings, and body sensations.

Context is the backdrop, or container the content exists within.

It helps to see this as an image, so here is a table to illustrate what I mean:

CONTENT	CONTEXT
Sound	Silence
Movement	Stillness
Physical objects	Space
Thoughts, emotions, body sensations	Pure consciousness

If we take sound to begin with. You can only identify that a sound is occurring, because of the context of silence underlying the sound.

It's the same with movement. You can only discern that movement is happening, because of the context of stillness.

And also, with physical objects. In order for us to have physical objects, we must have the context of space to house them in. For example, in our living rooms there is a space that furniture and people inhabit. The space always has to be greater than the objects to fit them all in.

We go about our everyday life, only paying attention to all the people and objects in our immediate surroundings. We miss a lot of the objects too, because our attention flits from one object or person to the next, with no awareness, or appreciation for the space in between everything.

This means we are then limited to that which we can be aware of. If the other person in front of us is angry, we get triggered by their emotional state because there is no awareness of space, to put the feeling into context. We become overwhelmed by our senses and overloaded with information with no way of making any sense of it.

This happens with sounds as well. I know a lot of people who get aggravated by certain sounds, or sounds that are too loud. They have lost conscious awareness of the context of silence, to balance out their experience.

It's the same with movement. It can be disorientating for some people to experience too much activity or movement near them.

This is why it's so important to start to consciously explore the context of stillness, silence, and space.

It is grounding and stabilising to become consciously aware of the context in life. Context is pure consciousness and you are that. It is conscious awareness which continues to look out through your eyes, as your body changes and grows older.

The context is the still, silent, unchanging part of ourselves and it is vast and infinite. When you are aware of that which does not move, that which is ever-present, it is like having an anchor to hold you steady when chaos ensues.

It also has the effect of reducing the intensity of the content, so it is no longer overwhelming.

We will always remain aware of the content, but it becomes bite-sized and manageable, maybe even enjoyable, when we have cultivated a conscious awareness of stillness and silence.

As we become more aware of the context, our perception of life expands so we are automatically able to see the bigger picture. We then experience life in a more gentle way, with a greater perspective of everything which is presented to us.

Chapter 19
The original blueprint

When you pay attention to the context of stillness and silence, you access the original blueprint. The original blueprint is the coding that your body follows to replicate itself to continually recreate healthy and functional bodily systems.

This blueprint gets overwritten by instructions from the mind and the emotional reactions to these thinking patterns. Every thought we have is an instruction to the body. This chaotic, negative thinking interrupts the original blueprint coding and the body starts to recreate itself based on these new instructions.

This is where the body starts to become dysfunctional. The messages from the mind are contradictory and continual. This puts an immense strain on the body, as it tries to keep up with all the different and often opposing instructions.

The body is designed to replicate in a healthy and functional way for ever. However, aging is accepted as a natural occurrence in today's society.

In the world today, the rate of aging is increasing. We are discovering different types of new diseases and the body is struggling to remain healthy from a younger and younger age.

Mental health is also an issue. It continues to become a greater and seemingly unsolvable problem. Allergies and sensory overload disorders are also on the increase.

This is partly because of the diet we eat, the lack of exercise, lack of daylight, and increasing stimulation and overload of information we are exposed to on a daily basis.

There is basically too much information going in for the mind and body to process. Some systems start to malfunction and slow down in efficiency, whilst other systems speed up to try and compensate. This leads to a whole host of complicated health conditions and symptoms which often Doctors cannot explain.

With the lack of understanding about why people are getting certain symptoms, new labels are being created to categorise these symptoms in an attempt to get a handle on them. But so often there is no remedy, other than medication and rest, which is largely ineffective.

We are not addressing our emotions or our thoughts as the source of the malfunction.

There is research going on in a scientific area called Epigenetics. Epigenetics investigates what factors affect our genes. We have short term, medium term and long term acting genes. These genes can be present in the body, yet not switched on.

Epigenetics research is discovering how many different factors have an impact on our genes, and how these factors switch particular genes on or off.

For example, you could have the gene for diabetes and if it never switches on, you will never experience the symptoms of diabetes. However, particularly with type 2 diabetes, more and more people are being diagnosed with this every day. The gene is being switched on and scientists want to find out why, to explore how to turn it off again.

This research is uncovering many different ways in which we alter our genetics, from external and internal sources. Externally the air we breathe, the food we eat, the chemicals we are in contact with, the stimulation from screens etc, all have an impact on our genes.

Internally we are affected by the content and quantity of thoughts we have. Also, by the intensity and frequency of our emotional reactions, with fight or flight chemicals being released etc.

In discovering all the factors which influence our genealogy, we are then able to develop ways to counteract the effects and reverse the symptoms.

We know we need to eat healthily and exercise, but we don't all do it.

One reason we don't all exercise could be we have become so overwhelmed by the quantity and intensity of thoughts and emotions. Thinking requires a lot of energy. We experience both thinking and emotions on a daily basis, and become so exhausted from all the internal activity, we don't have any energy left to exercise.

Our diet is not always entirely healthy, because most of us have learnt to eat to distract us from our emotions. We crave all sorts of foods and snacks to mask how we feel. There is a payoff from eating certain foods, which provide a hit of chemicals that make us feel good. So, when an uncomfortable or painful emotion comes up, we turn to food to change how we feel. Or a long list of other addictions. This can be a perpetual cycle which adds to the stress in our system and will most likely lead to further unhealthy habits.

In doing this we avoid confronting the emotion and it gets pushed down again and we feel ok for a while. Then it starts to rise again, as it always will and we have to eat something else, or find another way to feel better.

Avoidance causes the emotion to back up and intensify, coming up with more and more force each time. This leads us to up the ante, so to speak, and we eat even more, or turn to alcohol or another drug to combat the increased intensity.

When it becomes too intense to manage, it bursts out in the form of verbal, or physical violence. If we learn this is not acceptable, we become hostile and uncaring, or we choose another outlet, crying and victimhood.

All these reactions are unconscious, and we have little, or no control over how we react. People get angry with us and we become defensive. Thus, overloading our system further and our body suffers the consequences.

In order to come back to our original blueprint, it is essential we learn how to interrupt this downward spiraling pattern and change the unconscious process, to a more conscious one.

Then and only then do we actually have a choice about how we act and respond to other people's behaviour.

The only effective way I have discovered to interrupt this unconscious pattern, is to meditate. Meditation unravels all these patterns, allowing us to become conscious of what we are doing and saying. In becoming conscious of our thoughts and actions, we start to do things differently in a way that is in accordance with our true nature.

We cannot make any changes until we become conscious. We cannot see what is happening in our mind and the effect it has on our body, when it is an unconscious process. It is like we are asleep and not aware of what is truly going on.

But make changes we must, if we are to have a healthy, pain free experience of life.

The only question left to answer is:

'Are you willing to do something different, to change your current experience of life'?

We all want things to be better, happier, more peaceful. However, we don't all search for a solution, let alone implement it. We bitch and moan about the status quo and keep doing what we've always done. Obviously, (or maybe not so obviously for some) if you do the same things over and over, you will continue to get the same results.

Sometimes we do make external changes, but as this only addresses the symptoms and not the root cause, results are limited and unsustainable.

In order to make an effective and sustainable change, you must look in the only place left: within.

When you look within, you will find the unbroken you, whole and complete and waiting to be explored.

When you explore this inner still, silent self, then the game changes completely and a new, peaceful experience of life swiftly follows.

Part Three
Changing your relationship with pain

"These pains you feel are messengers. Listen to them."

"The cure for pain is in the pain."

"Don't get lost in your pain, know that one day your pain will become your cure."

"Through love, all pain will turn to medicine."

. . .

"I said: What about my eyes?
God said: Keep them on the road.

I said: What about my passion?
God said: Keep it burning.

I said: What about my heart?
God said: Tell me what you hold inside it?
I said: Pain and sorrow?
God said: Stay with it. The wound is the place where the Light enters you."

- Rumi -

Chapter 20
Meditation demystified

Meditation is the key practice, for bringing your attention within, to discover who you really are. It's important to find and consciously explore that still, silent part of yourself, which so often goes unnoticed. The outside world gets most of our attention.

Not all meditation practices are alike.

Many practices we call meditation are in fact just relaxation techniques. They are wonderful and we may gradually slow down and relax enough, so the mind will still. But it is a slow process and it is unlikely your everyday life will change that much by using these techniques.

They are very useful though, don't get me wrong. If you are stressed to the max and you learn one of these relaxation techniques, then it will definitely help you calm down a little. You will be soothed whilst you use the technique and the calmer state will flow into your day for a while.

But it won't change your relationship with your mind. The underlying cause for the stress building up, will still be operating behind the scenes and the stress levels will build back up again.

It's the same with guided meditation. Although some of these techniques will provide some changes within you, they won't go to the heart of the matter and cultivate sustainable change, which alters your entire perception and experience of life.

Another common and well know practice is mindfulness.

Mindfulness is great for starting to recognise the workings and mechanism of the mind, which will give you some clarity and space with all the thoughts and emotions passing through.

It is, however, all too easy to stay absorbed in the content of thought.

By this I mean you will be aware of the thoughts, which give you some space and will slow the activity in the mind, so you experience some calm. The mind can easily fool you though. You may think your mind is still, when in fact there is a quiet, subtle voice still commentating on, narrating, or analysing what you are observing.

This subtle dialogue will prevent you from experiencing absolute stillness and keeps the mind in play. Any activity in the mind puts a strain on your body and will create stress. It also uses up a lot of energy to maintain the activity of thinking.

One of the most common ways people meditate, is to follow the breath. It can be very calming to simply observe your breathing and slow it down, bringing your attention back into your belly, allowing the air coming in to expand and contract your stomach.

You can cultivate your health and calmness with the breath alone, bringing more oxygen in and creating movement assisting the body to heal and relax. It will bring about some great changes, yet it will still be a limited experience.

The main reason these types of meditation and mindfulness practices don't create fast and sustainable changes is, they keep your attention on content.

The most effective meditation techniques are ones that draw your attention inward mechanically. This is typically done by using a mantra, or phrase which replaces the other thoughts and brings your attention to the stillness underlying the movement of thought and emotion.

It's not just about what technique you use that makes a difference, it's also the way you use the technique. This is why a lot of people struggle to meditate on their own. In order to effectively overcome a lifetime's habit of excessively thinking, you will need guidance and feedback from someone who has stabilised their own experience of stillness; someone who is trained and qualified to teach you how to cultivate a relationship with stillness.

A lot of meditation teachers use guided meditation, which is wonderful to experience, especially in person in a group setting. This may be all you want out of a meditation practice. But there is so much more that an effective meditation technique can do for you with the right guidance and feedback.

Meditation can completely change your relationship with thought and emotion and even body symptoms. By 'changing your relationship', I mean you can have an entirely different experience of life. You will discover non-attachment.

When you are no longer attached to the content of thought, you are free. The thoughts no longer affect you. They can pass through your conscious awareness and not even touch your experience at all. This creates space for the useful, intuitive knowing to become visible as well, which makes life simpler and clearer.

It's the same with emotion. You can gradually train your response to emotion, by using the meditation techniques to redirect your attention back to the stillness, underlying the movement of emotion. As you gently but persistently use the techniques AND allow the emotional response to play out, you begin to clear out all repressed emotion. The tension in your body decreases, allowing your body to relax and heal more quickly. You will also activate a stable experience of stillness, which is calm and enjoyable and will act as an anchor when emotion bubbles up.

With less emotional stress stored in your cells, your body will work more efficiently and effectively. It will also be more efficient at maintaining good health and energy levels. Another happy side effect is, your mind will not be triggered into thinking incessantly. The need to try and work out why you feel a certain way and how to change the way you feel, will fall away.

With a more relaxed body, you will learn to allow the natural movement of homeostasis. The meditation techniques I use can dramatically change the way my physical body feels in a split second. One moment I can be in a world of pain and suffering, the next moment I can feel lighter and the pain vanishes. The amazing discovery is, although I can still feel the body sensations, I am able to move more freely with a fluidity and ease which is not there when the pain overwhelms me.

It's all about where your attention is in any given moment.

When your attention is on the dialogue about the painful body part, you want it gone and you fight with the sensations. When you use the technique and your attention moves to the space which exists within every cell in your body, the fighting ceases and your body relaxes, allowing healing to take place. The pain reduces or even dissipates completely, because all resistance has eased.

Resistance is the cause for the suffering and intensity of pain.

We were trained at a very young age to resist and now we do it automatically without even realising we are doing it.

Until we retrain ourselves to allow rather than resist, we will continue to suffer, experience pain and discomfort, and potentially a whole host of health issues.

A common misconception regarding meditation is, you have to stop your thoughts. The first meditation technique I learnt was counting to

10 and if a thought came in, I had to start again. This was very frustrating, and I doubt I even relaxed with this technique. I rarely got above 3 and I felt useless, because I could not stop the thoughts.

It is not necessary, or even useful to try and stop thinking. It uses effort. Effort always keeps us tense and away from an experience of stillness. There is a much easier and more simple way to have a direct experience of peace.

Meditation is a far more powerful and necessary tool than most people realise.

A lot of people think meditation is for hippies, or new age people. It's also a common belief that meditation is boring or impossible to do. When in fact, with an effective technique and an experienced teacher, it is very easy to learn and practice.

It is also completely natural and down to earth to practice meditation. Think of it as a gym for the mind, in training to become more aware.

You aren't taking yourself to a peaceful place outside of yourself by meditating. You are in fact just recognising the space within yourself where peace already exists.

The meditative state is your natural state of being, where nothing needs to be added, or taken away, to experience peace.

Chapter 21
Ascension techniques

Ascension is the practice I personally use and also teach. There are many reasons why I use this practice rather than any meditation or mindfulness practice. The main one being it is incredibly effective and yet also very simple and easy to use.

Ascension is similar to meditation, but the experience of the practice and accompanying teaching, although incredibly simple, goes far beyond the reaches of most meditation practices.

I have tried many meditation techniques over the years and I always used to struggle with them. I sometimes felt calm or peaceful, but I certainly didn't experience much change in my everyday life, as a result of the time I spent meditating.

The Ascension techniques are mechanical and therefore automatically and systematically do the work for you. These techniques require absolutely no effort and because they are mechanical, they naturally retrain your entire mind/body system to work efficiently and effectively.

You don't even need to believe they will work for you. All you need is the willingness to give them a go and spend the 20 minutes 2 or 3 times a day using them. They work every time you use them, no matter what, but you do have to use them.

There is no need to visualise anything, breathe in a certain way, or do anything more than use the technique and then watch what happens next. It's so supremely simple. Deceptively so.

The mind will question them and try to understand how and why they work. But the mind will never be able to answer these questions. This is because the techniques, as the name Ascension suggests, take you beyond the workings of the mind. They lead you to a direct experience of peace, deep into an ocean of stillness, silence, and space.

The Ascension techniques are called Attitudes, probably because they literally change your whole attitude towards life and yourself.

The Ascension Attitudes are basically short sentence which act as a vehicle, taking you deep into the heart of stillness, of endless peace and silence, which we refer to as the Ascendant.

They do this by charming the surface level of the mind, so you are immediately drawn into the Ascendant and the mind settles down to a complete state of rest. The techniques are structured in such a way, they automatically bring coherence and harmony to your mind.

When the mind comes to a complete rest, the body follows and comes to a complete state of rest as well. Only when the mind rests fully, does your body rest fully. This is because of the mind/body connection.

The mind/body connection is a natural function of all humans. We can identify this connection by a simple exercise which I spoke about in a previous chapter. Here is a recap of the exercise: Imagine that I am cutting up a lemon and handing you a segment. Then imagine you are biting into the lemon segment. Your body reacts doesn't it? There is no lemon in reality, yet just the thought of biting into one activates the salivary glands as if you were actually physically doing it.

It's the same across the body. If you think an angry thought, your chest will tighten, or your jaw may clench, and your hand sometimes forms into a fist and tenses. Likewise, if you feel anxious about something, you will experience a tensing or intense feeling in the stomach.

Every thought you have creates a response in the body. You are literally giving it an instruction, with every thought you have. This is what the Ascension Attitudes capitalise on. The Attitudes are essentially the thought which replaces these everyday thoughts, and which direct the mind inwards to the still, silent centre.

When the body comes to a complete state of rest, its natural tendency is to heal and throw off stress and tension.

Healing in the body is an active state. The activity happens by itself and is then reflected in the mind. Activity in the mind is expressed as thoughts. So thoughts are ok and very much a part of the process of releasing stored stress.

When we notice the thoughts, or recognise we are thinking, we simply and gently come back to the Ascension Attitude, think it again and watch what happens next.

The Ascension Attitudes are structured in a way that brings the mind into a complete state of coherence, by uniting the two parts of the brain, the linear and the spatial. This harnesses the full power of the brain, which is then targeted towards a root stress in our life.

These techniques are taught at a primary course called a First Sphere. The First Sphere is typically taught over a weekend by two Ishaya monks, who are trained and qualified teachers of the Ascension Attitudes. They will guide you through the process of learning and using these techniques most effectively. Sometimes the First Sphere is taught over a series of evenings or mornings when the need arises.

At the First Sphere course you will learn four Ascension Attitudes that are based on Praise, Gratitude, Love and Compassion. These four techniques work together, to release the stress stored in our nervous system, quickly and easily.

I had never before experienced such a deep state of rest, until I learnt these techniques in February 2010. The techniques seemed so simple and unassuming. I was incredibly surprised when they had such an immediate and powerful effect on me.

By the end of the course I was so relaxed and refreshed. It was such a huge relief. Not to mention being an absolute delight!

What was even more surprising to me was, they continued to expand my awareness of peace. Even now my life continues to get easier and more enjoyable day by day, week by week and year by year. However good life gets, there is always more.

The practice of Ascension and the ongoing support from the Ishaya monks, completely and utterly changed my life for the better. It has provided so much more than just a bit of stress relief and more peace. I have found purpose and fulfilment.

I no longer operate in the same way. My attitude has changed. My perception has changed. I have access to a completely different mode of operation - 'presence'. My ego is fast fading away and I experience peace as an ongoing endless state. And yet I'm more me than I've ever been.

My anger has dissipated, and joy has increased a hundred-fold. My body is healthier and more flexible. I still have asthma and Symphysis Pubis Dysfunction, but both conditions are easing and changing almost daily. My asthma is now very mild and is experienced just as a little shortness of breath, rather than a full-on asthma attack like I previously battled with.

The Symphysis Pubis is still affecting my mobility, yet it has abated for long periods of time. Currently as I write this book, it has flared up again. But the last time I experienced this level of immobility, I was also in excruciating pain. Now I only experience a low ache if I physically overdo it. Plus, it does not interfere with my experience of peace and happiness. I do what I need to do to look after my body, but there is no suffering and very little, if any pain at all.

Practising Ascension always gives you exactly what you need in each and every moment. It's a powerful and effective tool to change your relationship with thought, emotion, and body sensations.

Ascension has been invaluable for changing my relationship with pain. In fact, I wouldn't want to live without it. The techniques give me something to do, when I feel overwhelmed, stressed or experience pain. But it's the consistent practice of Ascension which cultivates the sustainable changes.

It's an ongoing dance and sometimes I forget. However, I am so grateful because as soon as I remember, all I need to do is choose. I can simply think an Ascension Attitude and my attention is on stillness again. The pain eases and I'm present.

I now notice, when pain occurs, there is always dialogue going on in my mind. Dialogue, or thinking as we commonly call it, is usually a sign you are resisting the movement of healing taking place in the body. To think, your attention is taken into the past or the future. Only when the mind stills, are you present and attentive to this moment.

In my experience, when I am present, there is never any pain and certainly no suffering. There may be an awareness of a sensation in the body, but the associated pain and suffering are not present.

I have also discovered when I am struggling to walk, there is always dialogue in my mind. I notice quite quickly these days, pause, use a technique, and then wait and watch to see what happens to the state of my body. Most of the time the aching eases, the mobility increases, and I feel so much lighter.

The Ishayas' Ascension goes beyond belief. It gives you peace, happiness and so much more besides. You finally discover who (and what) you really are. When the mind is still and you are present, life is a glorious adventure, fulfilling, rewarding and delightful.

Information on how to learn Ascension is at the back of this book.

Chapter 22
Innocence and gentleness

There are two useful approaches to assist an effective meditation practice and create a more functional, flexible and pain free body. Innocence and gentleness.

So often we tense against pain, and fight with our thoughts and emotions, so we create tension and rigidity in the mind and body. We can get stuck in this approach and it causes the level of pain to intensify, which then locks our bodies into a rigid state of tension.

When attempting to change your experience of pain, it is very helpful to use innocence to break us out of the pattern we are locked into. Innocence can lead to changing the old pattern to a more functional and gentler one.

Innocence in this case means to approach the pain with no agenda and no judgement, or even an opinion of what you are currently experiencing. To wipe the slate clean and look at the pain with fresh eyes, as if you have no idea what you are witnessing.

Curiosity is a great way to become really innocent and open to meditation, allowing it to work for you. Curiosity keeps us exploring innocently, rather than trying to do 'it' well.

Pain can feel like it is locked in and immovable. It can often appear to intensify for no apparent reason.

But there is a reason. You will only discover the reason for yourself by observing, without trying to change anything. Be curious about what is occurring and willing to witness without the attachment of needing to change what you are witnessing.

Witnessing can be so much easier and more beneficial when we are innocent and open to what we are witnessing.

It is very common for people to start attempting to witness the workings of the mind, especially as part of a meditation practice, whilst they have a strong idea of what is about to happen next.

This will cause tension and strain, which will slow down the results and prevent you from letting go and resting in stillness and silence.

The truth is we don't know what is going to happen next. In our mind, in our body, or in the world around us. But that doesn't stop our mind from having an opinion and continually commentating on what could or should happen next.

An innocent approach can free you from the chains of the mind's opinion of the situation at hand. It allows you to access a different experience. When the opinion of what is happening is no longer present, you get to experience this moment more purely and clearly, without the past effecting what you see and feel.

This makes your experience soften and allows movement in the body, cultivating a more enjoyable and gentle experience. More space is also a result of being innocent. The mind fills all of your attention, so it feels chaotic and busy. Innocence calms down the mind and creates space to experience things differently.

Another useful approach is gentleness. When you are gentle with yourself and in your approach, you find everything naturally slows down and your awareness expands. You also create space for intuitive recognition and a fluid, more graceful experience.

Here is a great little exercise to give you a clearer idea of how to be gentle, and to demonstrate (as an experience) what difference gentleness can provide.

First you will need to find a small object you can easily hold in your hand. Something like a pen is ideal.

In a sitting position, place the pen on your lap. Then simply pick it up and put it down again. Repeat this 3-4 times.

Then pause and this time pick the pen up and put it down, trying to be as gentle as possible. Repeat this 3-4 times trying to be even more gentle each time.

Then pause again and acknowledge what differences you noticed when you were being gentle picking the pen up. How did it feel different? Usually I do this exercise in person and allow people to discover their own answers. But as this is a book, I will give you a few of the answers people typically tell me.

Firstly, people notice that being gentle, whilst picking the pen up and putting it down again, slows the whole process down. They also report it gives them more space and also a more expanded awareness. It can also cultivate a greater level of alertness and attentiveness.

After using this exercise, I then get people to meditate with their eyes closed, so they can put what they have just learnt about gentleness into practice. Typically, everyone has a more still and deep meditation after using this simple yet effective exercise.

Gentleness is such a powerful and effective way to refine and deepen a meditation practice. It is also an important and useful approach when dealing with intense pain, or restriction in the movement of the body.

When you notice you are in pain and it is starting to overwhelm you, stop for a moment. Then allow your body to soften, to open up and gently allow the body to relax by itself. Watch and give a little space, to allow your body to unravel and relax little bit by little bit.

As you begin to move, make sure every movement is soft and gentle. Try moving slowly and paying attention to your movement, so you can adjust your movement when necessary. Allow the body to work within its current level of capability.

So often we move about in a tense and forced manner, which can cause the body undue strain and unnecessary wear and tear. Bringing a gentle approach into every movement, will ensure you don't force the body into a movement that will potentially put it under strain, or even cause damage.

Being gentle, slows everything down and brings more awareness into how we move. Body movement becomes more graceful and easy. It also creates space for intuition to let us know if we need to rest for a while and how long to rest for. We can begin to recognise particular movements which force the body and also discover that a small shift can ease the strain on the body. This allows us to move more effectively and efficiently, working with the restriction, or limitation our body is currently experiencing.

It's such a simple thing to do and yet it makes all the difference in the world.

If you are in pain, you will have learnt many habits which cause strain on the body. Habits that can take quite some time to be overthrown. Just as it took many years and lots of repetition to create and maintain our current habits, so it will take time, persistence, and repetition to cultivate new and healthy habits. Ease and functionality of movement will naturally develop, as you continue to practice this new approach.

Cultivating a new habit of innocence and gentleness, will support your body to re-balance itself and kick-start the natural process of homeostasis within your body.

It will make your experience of this moment more enjoyable and less painful, enabling you to move more freely and easily. You will also find as you sit down, you can gently adjust your position as required and prevent more tension being stored in your body. Thus providing you with a greater level of rest and recuperation, whilst you are sitting down.

One thing I found invaluable with my lack of mobility, poor core strength and rigidity, was looking at how I got up from a chair or sofa.

Again, gentleness was a big component of this process. I would look at what was available near me to help me pull myself out of the chair. Repositioning myself if necessary, before I attempted to get up. Then I would remind myself to move gently and slowly.

It could still be painful and require a great deal of effort. But as I practised gentleness, and accepted this was the way it was, I found there were lots of creative ways that could make the job easier.

It's also very important to be humble enough to ask for help. If using support from another person will make getting up less of a strain on your body, love yourself enough to ask for that help! It took me a long time to do this, because it felt humiliating and frustrating for me to be reliant on another person.

The first step is to receive the help when it is offered. Even if you don't think you need help. Receive it anyway. You may find the interaction with the other person is enjoyable and gives you a sense of connection that so often seems elusive when you are living in a world of excruciating pain.

As I got better at this and more open and willing to receive help, I often discovered I could be of service in return.

There are many ways to help, or give gratitude, when your body is not functional. But you will only discover them when you stop fighting the current state of your body.

I highly recommend you cultivate a gentleness in every move you make. Continually come back to innocence again and again.

Let this moment be brand new and be open to it being different than the last moment. Only with innocence is there space and possibility for change to happen. We become flexible and willing, which allows a positive change to develop.

Chapter 23
Commitment

The word commitment used to put me off doing things. It so often felt like it was loaded with pressure and the threat of failure.

This was until I read a short piece of text written by William Hutchinson Murray (1913-1996), from his 1951 book entitled The Scottish Himalayan Expedition.

This is the piece of writing in question:

. . .

"Until one is committed, there is hesitancy, the chance to draw back, always ineffectiveness. Concerning all acts of initiative (and creation), there is one elementary truth, the ignorance of which kills countless ideas and splendid plans: that the moment one definitely commits oneself, then Providence moves too. All sorts of things occur to help one that would never otherwise have occurred. A whole stream of events issues from the decision, raising in one's favour all manner of unforeseen incidents, meetings and material assistance, which no man could have dreamt would have come his way. I have learned a deep respect for one of Goethe's couplets:

Whatever you can do, or dream you can, begin it.
Boldness has genius, power and magic in it!"

. . .

This text was on the back of the door in all the rooms on my 'Mastery of the Self Course' in 2012, so I ended up reading it pretty much every day for 6 months.

At first it made me feel uneasy, because I didn't believe I was good at committing to anything and seeing it through to the end. I was very good at procrastinating and avoiding doing tasks that meant sticking my neck out and being seen.

I attempted to ignore it. But because it was in front of me every single day, I found myself reading it through over and over again.

After a few weeks it started to make me feel hopeful and even excited. There was still doubt I could achieve anything I wanted to. However, it was starting to make me feel empowered and open to the possibility I could do what I desired and get great results, if I committed myself fully to something.

It also started to sink in that the reason I had often not achieved the results I wanted, was because I didn't actually commit to it. My self-doubt caused hesitancy and scattered thinking and actions. If this was the case, I could change my approach and therefore change the outcome.

The seed was sown and has continued to have an impact on me.

Commitment is a very powerful thing. When we are committed to something it leaves no room left for doubt or hesitation.

It's also very easy to do. It's a simple decision and then we stick to it. If we fall down and stop committing, we can simply hit the reset button and recommit again.

Commitment is something we always suggest to people when they come to learn the Ascension techniques. We suggest it at the beginning of every course, as a means to create a more effective meditation practice.

And it works.

When you commit to something wholeheartedly. You stay on track more easily and you get much better results.

Commitment also cultivates a one-pointed focus that cuts out all distractions and maintains momentum in whatever task we commit to.

When we learn something new, it can be exciting at first but can quickly fall away after a few weeks, or even after a few days. Making a commitment and applying a time frame to the commitment, ensures you keep going with the task in hand.

The world lines up to support us in our endeavours when we commit to something, anything. Opportunities we may never have seen come our way with seemingly little or no effort. We slip into the natural flow of abundance and each step along the way shows up as if by magic.

I've always been a very determined person. When my mind was set on something, I worked very hard to find a way to achieve it. I was great at working hard and having no breaks, with the sole focus of getting a job finished. I used to mistake determination for commitment, but they are not the same thing.

Practising the Ascension techniques gave me the clarity to see where my determination worked against me. I often worked until I dropped and gave myself no time to rest or even pause to drink, eat, or take stock of what I had achieved so far. This approach was not sustainable, and I discovered this the hard way.

My hard work ethic was often praised by those in authority and so it made me redouble my efforts to please these people, gaining the respect and admiration of everyone.

Eventually this took its toll on my body and it gave way to a state of absolute exhaustion and I was diagnosed with ME.

Often ME is called chronic fatigue syndrome and people who are diagnosed with either of these conditions can be thought of as lazy.

I gradually recovered enough to carry on a normal life. But I still had a determined streak that tripped me up again and again.

Determination meant I kept to my Ascension practice, but it often led to me using effort and force, which prevented the techniques from being as effective as they could be.

Learning about commitment and what that truly meant, gave me the capacity to maintain my practice without using effort or force. This very quickly refined my experience of stillness and peace. It also has allowed me to start and finish, pretty much everything I choose to do.

Commitment makes life easier, opens up channels of support and brings opportunities to us that otherwise do not manifest in our life.

There is a boldness which appears in our experience when we commit. Power and momentum are initiated, and magical things come our way.

Commitment also brings fulfilment and reward with it, so life is more enjoyable, even before you complete what you set out to do.

Commitment, rather than determination, means my passion can flow and I am more flexible in my approach. I can therefore adjust course if, or when, required.

I find I rarely get distracted by things that are not of any use. I no longer waste so much time on pointless tasks leading nowhere. I am more aware of possibilities and opportunities which can support my current project.

I have also found intuition becomes a greater guiding force when I commit to something.

My mind naturally slows down, allowing intuition to take over and lead the way. There is space for the relevant thoughts, which support my ideas and bring them to fruition, to be heard and acted upon.

With my health issues, commitment to being present has provided many resourceful options to be revealed and utilised. This has cultivated a better state of health. I have discovered so many ways to combat pain, and to change the relationship with my mind and body.

I am now in tune with what my body needs, without getting stuck in a course of action that stops being productive, or helpful.

Commitment is a very useful approach indeed.

Chapter 24
Surrender

Surrender is simply giving up the fight. This is not about surrendering to another person; it is an inner quest of surrendering the inner battle that takes place in your mind.

Surrender is the same as allowing and also letting go.

The most powerful thing to surrender is your thoughts. The need to think is a dominant pattern and most of us are literally addicted to thinking. Thinking keeps our attention on either the past or the future.

In order to be present, you will have to surrender the need to think.

This will be difficult for some to comprehend, because we have been trained to think. We were trained by our parents, by our schools and by the rest of society. We use the mind to discern what is right or wrong and subsequently we remain submerged, in a mind created version of reality.

We can very easily miss, or misunderstand what is actually happening around us, because we are paying attention to the commentary about what is happening. We have an auto translate mechanism which interprets what our senses are experiencing, based on the belief system stored in our subconscious mind.

What we see and hear, taste, touch, and smell, pass through the internal filters of the mind. These filters inform us of what we are seeing, hearing, tasting, touching, or smelling.

The first time this actually sank in as a truth was a startling discovery and took a while for me to fully comprehend.

It was tricky to comprehend, because we believe what we are experiencing is the truth. We believe the information we perceive is accurate, complete and all we have access to. Most of what we experience is, in fact, only the mind's interpretation of what it believes to be true.

I discovered the impact my mind had on my senses, on a day when I was not wearing my glasses. I had taken my glasses off, in order to give my eyes a rest, because I had been experiencing frequent and severe headaches for a while. Someone had suggested it may be my glasses causing the headaches. I checked with my optician and he agreed this could be the reason.

I started to take my glasses off for periods of time. For example, when I was at home and didn't need to see clearly.

One day I was cuddling my husband and we were chatting and laughing together, enjoying each other's company. I glanced over his shoulder at the digital clock on the cooker and I noticed the numbers were crystal clear. I gasped! But as I told my husband, the numbers instantly became blurry again.

I stopped in my tracks and blinked a few times, but the numbers remained blurry. My vision had been clear for long enough to realise if I could see clearly, even for a brief moment, then my eyes could not be faulty. My vision became blurry again, only when my mind kicked back in and I recognised that I could see clearly. The blur happened in my mind.

It was as if my mind was operating a programme that disabled my eyesight and caused blurred vision.

This moment had a great impact on me, which led to a great deal of research into how the eyes actually worked.

I found a whole host of books by people who had retrained their eyesight. A common theme in these books was the concept of clear vision being something that naturally comes to you, when you relax and stop trying to see.

So, what has this got to do with surrender? In the moment I could see clearly, I was relaxed and playful. There was no thinking occurring in my mind. It was still and I was present, enjoying the moment, and this allowed my eyes to function naturally, with no instructions from the mind to operate differently.

Surrender is a natural state of being. It's not so much something you do, as something which happens when you stop doing.

The doing I'm referring to here, is the activity in the mind. Most of the activity in the mind is unconscious, so we don't recognise it is taking place.

Meditation is the best tool for accessing this natural state of a still, clear mind. Which, in turn, allows for the natural functioning of movement in the body. Movement that keeps us alive and healthy.

To access a still mind and become present, we need to surrender the activity in the mind. Said another way: we allow the natural activity of the body to happen, so it can function effectively. Or another way to say it is, we can let go of the need to think, so we can tune in and become aware of the natural flow of life.

Letting go can be a confusing concept. It suggests doing something and so we try and try to let go, but instead we end up intensifying the discomfort, or pain, in our efforts to let go.

I often describe the letting go process as a letting it be, or letting it in. For example, when we are tense and in pain, we can notice where we feel the tension and give the body the instruction of allowing the natural movement of that part of the body to happen. To let it be exactly as it wants to be, and then let all the natural impulses rise within us and release through us, up and out.

A useful way to look at it, is to simply acknowledge we are resisting 'what is'. In acknowledging this resistance, we stop fighting against 'what is' and let our experience be exactly as it is right now.

Just by doing this, we relax a little and gain some perspective on our current experience. It provides the space to attain some clarity on what is actually occurring within us.

Using acknowledgement as a steppingstone to surrender, makes the whole process easier and more manageable.

The internal fight can only continue in the shadows. The moment we become aware of this internal activity in our mind, the mind slows down and stops all by itself. The mind requires our attention and permission to continue thinking.

Meditation is therefore an essential tool, in cultivating awareness and retraining the mind to slow down and still.

The Ascension techniques are the only tools that have continually, consistently, and effectively changed my relationship with thought. I no longer identify myself as the thinker of the thoughts.

A still mind is so delicious and enjoyable to experience. When you discover and learn how to do this, you are soon motivated to continue using the techniques, in order to stabilise and sustain this natural state of being.

It's a no brainer. Once you taste stillness as an experience, rather than just a theoretical concept, you will never want to go back to the chaos and busyness of the thinking mind again.

Surrendering thought back to stillness, is simple enough. Yet the mind can throw up all sorts of decoys and traps that lead us to believe we are surrendering.

In my experience it requires the guidance of someone who has already identified these traps. Firstly, to help you to recognise when the mind has kicked back in and has found a way to fool you, and secondly, to help guide you back to a direct experience of stillness and silence.

With ongoing guidance, you will begin to spot these traps on your own and learn how to allow the mind to still by itself.

The rule is, if it feels hard (or less than easy), ask for help. To come back to the simplicity and ease of a meditation practice, you will need the support and guidance from a person who has the experience and understanding of how to achieve this.

Meditation is easy when you know how. It's easy when you apply the simple instruction. But the mind is crafty and often extremely subtle. Only someone who has already stabilised their own experience can help you in this process.

Once you become more practiced at meditating, you can then use the techniques to change your relationship with the pain and suffering.

I have taught many people to ascend, some whom have experienced pain dissipate naturally and easily all by itself. Sometimes it only softens and eases a bit. But with ongoing guidance, one can learn to consciously use the techniques to allow your body to heal and function more efficiently.

Pain then becomes a choice. Nobody will consciously choose for pain. So, when pain comes calling, you apply the instruction and choose instead for peace.

Thankfully, it gets easier with practice.

Chapter 25
Ending the need to do something

We are human <u>beings</u>, yet so often we have learnt we need to <u>do</u> something in order to validate ourselves.

This is because we believe deep down, there is something wrong with us. This belief creates the drive to continually look for a way to improve ourselves, so we can be acceptable to others. Essentially to prove we are in fact good enough.

The mind is therefore activated to find a solution, a way to be better. Then and only when a satisfactory solution has been found, will we be, liked, loved, appreciated, accepted. And also, safe.

This is a lie.

A lie that keeps us beholden to the need to think and continually do things to make us feel good enough.

Because it's a lie, we never actually ever fulfil the need. As the need is never fulfilled, it perpetuates the pattern of thinking and doing... forever.

That is, until we become wise to this dysfunctional pattern and learn how to override and delete it.

In order to delete this pattern, it is necessary to go to the root of the matter. To change this habit of a lifetime, you will need to create a pattern interrupt, which will stop the pattern from being sustained. Then we can activate a new pattern. One that fulfils our every need and is natural. Natural means it will also be sustainable.

Awareness is essential in changing this pattern. We cannot change anything, if we are not aware of what we are doing in the first place.

One of the best ways to become aware of dysfunctional patterns of thinking and behaviour is to simply pause and pay attention.

The importance of the pause is recognised by practising it. Pausing allows you to begin to see more, to spot the automatic thinking we don't usually notice, simply because we are so involved in it. Habitual thinking is mostly unconscious, so we have no awareness of a large percentage of the thought streams flowing through our minds.

Yet all these unconscious thought streams are governing our day to day existence. I don't know about you, but when something has such a dominant effect on my life, I want to make sure it's based on my conscious choices. In short, I want a say. I want to be able to consciously choose what I decide is right for me.

Choice gives us freedom and also allows us to relax. When you don't feel pressurised or forced into a decision, or action, your body is better able to relax and release tension.

The need to do something to validate ourselves is exhausting and it is stressful.

Being able to step back from the dialogue, telling us how to live our lives, what is wrong, or what could go wrong, is invaluable.

We need to eat and drink. We need to have clothing and shelter, and we need human company to thrive. But beyond the essentials necessary for our survival, there is very little else we actually need.

There are of course things we want and it's good to have a desire, something to focus on, to inspire us to participate fully in life. To continually grow as a human being, and find a sense of purpose, is what gives meaning to our daily life.

When you derive a sense of meaning and fulfilment from your actions, life is more relaxing, more contented, and more enjoyable. Discovering something that gives you fulfilment is essential to good mental and physical health. It then becomes a passion and motivation that will drive your actions, rather than a need to be validated.

When passion drives you, life is exciting and satisfying. The focus is positive and uplifting, which cultivates a productive and efficient approach.

The need to prove yourself will then fade away into the background. With less attention on this unnecessary, unconscious thinking pattern, it loses its charge and eventually will disappear altogether.

Another reason for combating the need to do something is to save energy! We use a lot of energy to maintain the thought and action driving the need for validation. This wasted use of energy, would be much better utilised for healing the body and energising your every move.

This need to do something to validate yourself, keeps your focus on what is wrong with you and the world around you. What we put our attention on grows, which means we perpetuate the idea and associated feeling there is something wrong with us. So not only are we wasting energy on a false belief, we are also ensuring this false belief continues to be maintained, taking up air space in our mind and governing our every thought, feeling and action.

Do you want to do this? Does it make sense to support this false idea and allow it to have power over your daily life? No, it does not.

Once you begin to understand what is occurring in your unconscious mind, you can then choose to learn how to change these unconscious patterns and begin a new habit. A habit which will bring everything from the unconscious, into conscious awareness. This new habit will provide you with the ability to govern your own words and behaviour, in a way that makes sense to you.

In part four, I will give you practical tips and actionable exercises, to cultivate a greater sense of clarity and awareness, which will give you a new focus to shape your life in a more positive direction.

These exercises will give you a direct experience of a quiet and grounded state, that will lead to a more rested, functional, and healthy body.

Anything and everything which supports your body's natural tendencies to heal and to operate more efficiently and effectively, will allow healing to take place in every area that is painful, or functioning poorly.

It can be a dance back and forth, with the old habits attempting to re-assert themselves again and again. But with persistence and commitment to creating a new, more natural habit, you will begin to see the difference. Once you see even a small difference, it will inspire you to continue with the new regime.

Chapter 26
Emotional awareness / connection

We often think of the physical body as a separate entity to emotions and thoughts. In truth, it is impossible to define where one ends and the other begins. The physical body, thought and emotion are intrinsically linked in a way that is hard to fathom.

To ignore our emotions is to ignore our self. Ignoring is like building a wall inbetween you and that which you want to ignore. Your attention is still on 'it'. 'It', therefore, has all the power and this will limit you.

We have trained our whole lives to ignore our emotional responses. To push down certain feelings, to control our reactions and 'behave' in a certain way.

To voice how we feel has been judged as wrong, unacceptable, silly, unimportant amongst other things. We haven't been allowed to say how we feel in so many situations, in so many different ways that we have forgotten what we wanted to say in the first place.

Humiliation, threat and even punishment, has ensured we have become very proficient at hiding how we truly feel.

When we're not allowed to be ourselves, we have to find ways to internalise our emotions. This is toxic to our state of mind, our emotional state and, of course, to our physical state.

For the past ten years, I have been discovering in many ways and on many different occasions, with many different people, I don't allow myself to respond in a way that feels natural to me.

I discovered quite a few years ago now, I had learnt to edit my natural impulses and words. I found I would notice what I had said and then I would realise it was not congruent with what I felt, or what I consciously held to be true.

Initially I said nothing about my edited words. But after a while I started speaking up and saying things like "I don't know why I said that". Or "I don't even think that, and I certainly don't mean it that way!"

I used to feel like I had to stick with what I had initially said. Almost as if it was wrong somehow to call myself out and say what I really felt, what I really meant.

Now I'm completely honest with myself and this allows me to be completely honest with others. It's not that I intentionally lied. I had just learnt if I said what I really felt, I would get into trouble. So I had to find ways to communicate, in a way that kept the peace with the people around me. I did this so I would not be humiliated, shouted at or punished.

It was the same with my emotional responses. I started to notice how my body would almost freeze and I would hold my breath.

Gradually, over time, I have become able to spot this response very quickly and allow the emotion to pass.

I also began to notice I was clenching my jaw for no apparent reason. Or my shoulders would be raised and tense. These examples are only the beginning of my body's defence system, the list goes on. The body is simply following the instruction from my fearful thought patterns and gradually freezing up to supposedly remain safe.

These days I am much more aware, of my body, of my emotions and of my thoughts.

At any given moment, if I notice I feel uncomfortable, or a part of my body is sore, tense, painful or weak, I am able to recognise I am holding in and repressing a feeling or sensation.

There appears to be no difference if the tension is caused by an emotional feeling or a physical sensation. Either way I can notice it, watch it, and pay attention as my body softens and relaxes.

What I have found, is this has become really obvious and easy to do when I'm sitting down, or don't have a particular task to carry out immediately. But the minute I'm involved in a task, the habit to clench my jaw, or hunch my shoulders for example, reasserts itself. This is because the habit is so deeply ingrained, and my attention is occupied by the task I'm focused on.

You can learn to retrain this habit quite easily though. You can learn to become more aware of the resistance to and repression of your emotions. It doesn't involve being on high alert. It doesn't involve concentration. In fact, it's quite the opposite.

Repression of emotion is something you do. You don't have to do something else to stop the repression. You simply become aware by pausing and paying attention.

An effective way to become more aware is to learn the Ascension techniques. Partly because they cultivate alertness and partly because they retrain your mind, which automatically changes your relationship with thought and emotion.

Then all you have to do is allow the repressed emotion to pass through you, without controlling it. Easy, right?

Not always! It's easy once we see we are resisting the release of emotion. But we are so well trained at repressing emotion, we can't see we are holding on to it and identifying with it. It becomes the predominant experience, even though we are trying to hide from it. It seems like 'it', the emotion, is part of us. But 'it' is not part of us.

Repression alters and twists our emotions. What once was a small thing, pure and clear, becomes distorted and large, so much so we no longer recognise it for what it is.

Honest recognition of our emotional state allows the emotion to release, thus freeing us from future suffering.

We, as humans, do not liked to be forced. The only reason we force our emotions down, is because we were either threatened, ridiculed, or bribed into doing so.

Repression is forceful because it is not natural. No emotion is wrong. Anger only turns into rage when it is not allowed free passage. Sadness turns into grief when it is not given permission to be expressed.

Repression is unconscious and therefore it is difficult to spot. Gradually, as we become more aware, we become more conscious of this process. Then all we have to do is stop when we notice we are repressing something. In fact, it changes from repression to suppression when we become conscious of our responses, because suppression is a conscious behaviour.

We have no control over repression, but we do have control over suppression. Becoming conscious is therefore an important part of this process of letting go.

Becoming more emotionally aware, is the foundation for changing our emotional state. You cannot change what you are not aware of.

Changing your emotional state is key to changing your physical state. It would appear the body will always heal and rebalance when repression of emotion ceases.

This may not be true for everyone, but it has been proven to be true, in my experience, over and over again.

An effective way of encouraging emotion to express and pass through you, is to feel it 100%. When you feel an emotion 100%, no editing, no changing any part of it ... it moves. An emotion has a beginning, a middle and an end. It is finite and will not go on forever. So, feel the emotion fully and it will pass.

One trick which will assist you in allowing an emotion, is to breathe. As I mentioned before, I had begun to notice I was holding my breath. When you hold your breath, the emotion cannot move. You literally stop the emotion in its path when you hold your breath.

The antidote is, of course, to simply breathe. If we're not holding our breath, then we may be experiencing shallow breaths up into the chest area, which reduces our oxygen intake and prevents movement in the belly.

We tend to hold a lot of stress in our belly and so the tension prevents the diaphragm from moving down in its natural rhythm. It is therefore forced to move up instead of down, so we can still manage to maintain breathing and remain alive.

In part four I have dedicated a whole chapter for breath exercises, so you can explore them all and experiment with which works the best for you.

Cultivating emotional awareness will also lead to greater and more long-lasting connection with other human beings.

As you become more comfortable in your own skin, less reactive and more grounded in peace, you will naturally and more easily be able to connect and bond with your friends and family.

When we get along with all the other people in our lives, we tend to experience more happiness and contentment. We also enjoy interactions more fully, have fun and relax our posture and breathe more deeply.

We don't tense and repress our emotions when we're happy and having fun. The body is more relaxed and therefore this improves the natural functioning of the body, so it can heal and operate effectively and efficiently.

Stress can also be released though joy and laughter, just as easily as crying and sadness.

Emotional release does not need to be uncomfortable or difficult. There need not be any suffering.

In fact, when we allow ourselves to 'feel' whatever we feel, it moves through us with ease, leaving us feeling softer and lighter.

Sadness can turn to joy in a heartbeat. Anger, or hate, can turn to love in the blink of an eye. Often nothing need be said to achieve this change. To another, or to our self.

Just watch and allow, this too will pass.

Chapter 27
Find peace in the pain

The idea of finding any peace in the pain used to really confuse and frustrate me. This was partly because I didn't believe it was true and had plenty of experience with pain to back up my belief.

Pain was something that happened regularly. When pain happened, which it inevitably would, I just took a tablet and it eased or disappeared.

Until it didn't. Until I took a tablet and the pain remained. So, I took two tablets which worked for a while. Then when that stopped working, I took three tablets.

This approach was clearly not sustainable, and I realised medication was no longer an option which achieved the desired results. In my early twenties I started researching alternatives. I read somewhere pain relief medication caused headaches. Well! As that was my number one complaint, it made no sense to take them anymore. So, I stopped.

Then after more research I stopped taking antibiotics, antihistamines, throat capsules etc. The only two remaining were the birth control bill and my asthma inhalers. Then when my husband and I started a family, I stopped taking the pill and attempted to reduce the need for an inhaler.

I became healthier initially. But my body had another plan. Forget the headaches, coughs, sore throats and colds and instead, during the pregnancy of my second child, it turned to something else - Symphysis Pubis Dysfunction.

After the birth, this condition should have gone away by itself. But it did not. The pain was a whole new level of agony which made migraines pale in comparison.

I was prescribed increasingly stronger pain relief tablets, until I was given a Morphine derivative.

As I said before, the Morphine medication worked the first time I took it and the relief was a godsend. However, the second time I took it, I couldn't move from my bed. I was dizzy and disorientated and could not function at all. Plus, the pain relief was minimal.

I never used Morphine again. And for that I am very grateful.

Fast forward a few years, and after trying a range of different remedies and therapies, I was practising the Ascension techniques. My pain levels reduced naturally as a by-product of Ascending and life was so much easier.

Until it wasn't. Until pain reared its ugly head and caught me in its grasp again. This is when I actively started exploring what Ascension could do for the pain.

My first approach was, of course, to get rid of the pain. I didn't know how to go about doing this, so I asked for help from a Bright Path Ishaya teacher.

I explained I had pain and it was becoming more intense and asked how I could make it go away.

The first answer I got was to allow the pain to be there. Well that didn't go down too well! I asked what else I can do. It was suggested I put my attention 'in' the pain and use the Ascension technique from 'there'.

I was open to trying anything and had already learnt to trust The Bright Path Ishaya teachers, so I gave it a go.

It didn't work. The pain just intensified and became more and more unbearable. So, I asked another teacher and another, again and again and again.

Sometimes what the teacher suggested worked, sometimes it did not. Often, even if it did work initially, there would always come a time when the suggested approach or technique appeared to stop working.

At some point, I came across a Rumi quote - "The cure for pain is in the pain." I didn't understand what this meant, and it didn't really make much sense to me at the time. But it did get me thinking... and I came back to those words again and again, curious as to what they meant. Curious as to how finding out, might make a difference to my experience.

In pondering upon this Rumi quote, it occurred to me we are mostly empty space. Though we appear so dense and solid, that this idea seemed to run contrary to my experience of the body. The pain and body symptoms seem to be so rigid, locked in and immovable. But it piqued my interest.

Essentially, in exploring this concept, I naturally slipped into witnessing the body. In doing so, my body would begin to either gradually soften and relax, or a rather startling and exciting thing would occur - the symptoms would disappear in an instant.

When the latter happened, it didn't feel startling in the moment it actually happened. In fact, when the symptoms would disappear in a flash, it felt like a perfectly natural and normal thing to happen.

Presence is such a full experience that even if something happened only seconds before, it simply no longer registered or even appeared to have existed.

Gone ... 'poof!' without a trace.

This was fascinating to the mind, which could not comprehend what was going on! The startled reaction only kicked in when the mind had re-engaged again.

As I played with this concept and observed these changes occurring, I began to see the patterns I had been carrying out for decades. Patterns in my thinking, patterns in my emotional reactions and patterns in my physical body.

This observation simplified the whole process for me. Rather than having a whole host of different symptoms and areas of my body where I held tension, with lots of different muscle groups, it became apparent the solution, or cure, was in fact 'in the pain'.

I no longer needed to search for lots of external cures and ways to ease the symptoms. All I needed to do was watch and allow the movement of healing to happen. That's it - watch and allow.

Then peace reveals itself, even if the symptoms are still there. The intensity and tension eases and softens ... and suffering ceases.

I came to the realisation; I had understood the answer back to front. I wanted health, peace, freedom, joy, and I was searching for all these things on the outside, somewhere else, in another time and place.

As long as I needed the pain to go, it would stay. When I stopped needing it to go, when I stopped trying to heal my body and just observed the pain, then the peace and health, freedom and joy was revealed right here, right now,

In that moment I ceased looking in the wrong place. I ceased needing for something to change, or to be fixed in order to experience peace.

When I stopped searching and needing to be fixed, the peace could at last be discovered. And, in that present state of peace, my body could unravel the tension and holding-in patterns to heal itself.

And that felt really lovely!

Peace does exist in the pain.

This statement will torture you as long as it is an alien concept to you.

So, make friends with it. Explore with an open mind, the possibility of any truth in that statement, and use the toolbox of tricks described in part four, to unwrap the gifts pain has hidden in its depths.

You don't have to believe it to be true.

All it takes is curiosity, hope and the willingness to try a different approach.

Be willing to answer the question for yourself.

"Is there peace in the pain?"

Be willing to explore and experiment with the exercises in this book. And, be open to change.

In my experience, the systematic approach of the Ascension techniques is also invaluable. They have been the foundation for changing my relationship with pain.

Chapter 28
Prioritise your peace

What you focus on grows, as I've said before. So, it is of the utmost importance you switch your focus from pain to peace.

This can be easier said than done, because we are very well trained at focusing on what is wrong, so we can put it right.

If you want to change your relationship with pain, you will need to commit to prioritising your peace and stay as one-pointed as possible.

Our thinking follows the well-worn familiar pathways in the brain. In order to change these channels to new ones, you will need to be creative and persistent.

First and foremost, take a long look at your environment and begin to make changes, so it is congruent with peace.

A good place to start is the people in your life. The people we hang out with the most have a huge impact on our state of being.

One suggestion I have is to draw a line down the middle of a piece of paper to create two columns. In the left column write down the names of all the people in your life who make you feel good about yourself. The people who make you feel safe and loved, who support your choices, encourage, and appreciate you.

Then in the right-hand column, write down the names of all the people who make you feel bad about yourself. The people who make you feel uncomfortable, judged, or worthless. Who put you down, criticise and discourage you.

Take a good look at the list and consider stopping contact, or at least reducing the time spent with those in the right-hand column. If they're a family member or work colleague and you still have to see them, experiment with having less contact for a while.

This includes the thoughts in your head. There's no point in staying away from these people if you are going to continually think about them. So, if you catch yourself thinking about a right-hand column person, stop and change the subject, to someone or something which gives you pleasure.

The next area of your life to target is your home environment. Assess the space you live in and note down any changes that would make your personal space into a more relaxed, calm, happy, peaceful, and safe place. A place you will enjoy living in. Then implement as many of the ideas on your list as you can.

I started with organising my home, so it was easier to keep it tidy without too much effort. Once I had begun, I found various ways of being much more efficient and tidy were revealed. So quite quickly my home became a more peaceful haven and I felt more relaxed.

Colour coordination helped for me personally as well. When all the colours in the room matched, I found it had a soothing effect on me. Matching colours create more coherence in the mind.

I also have supportive cushions, a heat pad, massage tool and various other items that are all in reach of where I sit. This makes my life a lot easier when my mobility declines.

Pets are helpful as they love you unconditionally.

Be creative, have fun with it and work with what you've already got. You'll be surprised at what you discover in the process.

Work environments and anywhere else you spend quite a bit of time are useful to assess as well. Any area of your life which impacts on your daily routine, make sure that it supports you and is congruent with a calm and peaceful state.

If something you don't like, you find awkward or irritating cannot be changed, learn to accept it as best you can. See if you can find something you can appreciate about it. Be light-hearted as much as possible, because being serious sucks the joy out of everything and holds tension in the body.

Treat your whole world like it is one big mirror. Anything or anyone who shows a reflection you don't like, pause, and pay attention.

The world around you mirrors your inner unconscious mind. If someone is rude to you, it's likely you are holding a belief you are not good enough, in a way that matches their words or actions.

When someone like this upsets you, let it hurt, with no need to fight back or hide. Let it hurt. The sting of the feeling caused by their words or actions, is the old belief burning up in the fire of absolute truth.

I don't mean become a doormat and let people walk over you. Just don't jump to defend yourself. Let the words go through you and wash away the limiting patterns of belief. And certainly, don't put yourself in the presence of such people unnecessarily.

Just drop the fight or flight approach. Stand your ground and pay attention. Say what is there to be said, then let it go and move on. Notice what hooks your attention and limit exposure to anything that brings your mood down. Seek out everything and everyone who makes you feel happy and safe, positive and uplifted, supported and calm.

Create an environment and life you enjoy.

Take time for yourself. Rest when needed. Put yourself at the top of your to-do list and make sure all your needs are met.

You are important.

If you feel happy and peaceful, that will have a big impact on others. We are always more productive if we are happy.

Prioritise your peace.

Don't let anyone or anything get in the way of your peace. If you are paying something, or someone, a lot of attention, even if it is only in your head, then you are prioritising them. Does this thing or person make you happy? If the answer is no, then stop thinking about them, or hanging out with them and move on to pastures new.

Follow your heart. Do what feels right for you and avoid anyone who challenges your dreams. Or at the very least don't share your dreams with them.

Do this and you will begin to relax, your body will relax, and peace will become an easier choice to make.

If you have to do something that is stressful, uncomfortable, or difficult, choose to focus on it 100%. That way you will get the job done faster, you will have more clarity and it will be easier to complete.

Then when you have finished the stressful task, leave it in the past. Draw a line under it and step into the next job or activity with 100% of your attention. If you mind goes back to it, re-establish your focus on your new activity.

It's helpful to follow any unpleasant task with something you enjoy or find relaxing. Probably best it isn't food or alcohol, or something which can become addictive, or produce unhealthy side effects. I'm not saying not to, just be wary of the knock-on effects, of anything you may become reliant on to feel good or relax.

Choose something which is easy to do and will lift your mood, some activity you find enjoyable and relaxing.

If you have a whole day of tasks and activities you don't enjoy, endeavour to find some part of your day that is enjoyable. Again, be creative and playful in discovering what can make your day lighter, brighter and easier, even if only in a small way. Then focus on the good, as you go about your day.

Peace is your birthright. Prioritise peace in each and every moment.

Why?

Because you're worth it.

The world needs people who value themselves and who prioritise their peace. Peace is contagious. Fill yourself up with peace and spread it out into the world.

Every.

Single.

Moment.

Of.

Every.

Single.

Day.

Chapter 29
Pay attention

To pay full attention is something we rarely do. In a world with social media and 101 things vying for our attention every day, our attention flits from one piece of information to another. But we are not in control. It may seem like we choose to pick up our smart phone to look at something, or carry out a task, but it is all happening on autopilot.

How often do you find yourself on Facebook, Instagram, or YouTube, because a video, or article, caught your attention? One minute you are replying to an email or checking a notification and the next you are lost in a sea of cat videos, or other visual entertainment that interests you! If not social media, other areas of life have similar distractions.

You are not present, or conscious of what you are doing. You are automatically following the breadcrumbs and lose track of time, thus forgetting what you were meant to be doing.

This is not your fault. However, it is a time-wasting pattern which pulls you away from what is productive and useful.

Why does this happen? And why do we seem to be unable to stop it from happening time and time again?

It happens because we want to experience joy. The mind knows this and tries to direct you towards what it thinks will make you happy. Cat videos make me happy! But it's a quick fix that only lasts so long before it needs a top up. Plus, it distracts you from living a full and productive day.

Joy is our natural state of being and therefore is very easy to experience. I know it doesn't appear this way and is often elusive for long periods of time. But joy is a possibility in each and every moment. Even without social media, or YouTube videos!

True joy is only apparent when we are present. We have to actually show up in this moment, to recognise and experience joy. When we are thinking about that which makes us happy, it can feel good, but it pales in comparison to the joy you can feel when you are fully present.

The 'happy thinking' kind of joy is also only possible when we are thinking happy thoughts. The 'being present' kind of joy is a stable and ongoing state which only ends when you stop paying attention.

There is a big difference between paying attention to thought and paying attention to this moment as it unfolds. One is something we have been training to do our entire life and the other is a new uncultivated habit which requires some practice to maintain.

Yet paying attention to this moment is our natural state of being. It requires no effort and is a subtle shift of attention, away from thought; to the space, the conscious awareness that thought flows through. The backdrop so to speak. The void, or nothingness which is the underlying nature of reality.

This nothingness is indescribable and actually a very full and satisfying space to place your attention. It is nothing, or rather no-thing, no manifest thing or object. Yet it is the source of everything in existence, so it is alive, vibrant, and very enjoyable to experience.

It may be indescribable, but it is possible for everyone to experience this space for themselves.

And all you need to do is pay attention. Pay attention without judgement, without an agenda, without a need for this moment to be any different from how it is right now.

To pay attention fully, you have to be willing to give up control. You have to be willing to let the ebb and flow of life unfold, without trying to force it to be the way you think it should be.

It takes focus and alertness to maintain presence and be open to things being different in the next moment.

The controller in us wants to know what is going to happen in the future. It cannot let up for a minute trying to make sure everything is safe and going to plan.

Our plan always makes sense to us, but it doesn't take into account all the variables which can happen when we interact with others. We have a plan to keep ourselves safe and organised. It seems logical to do so and whilst it is useful to have a plan, it's necessary to be open and fluid to change when circumstances demand.

Being present is not only more enjoyable than the thinking state, it also provides us with a much bigger and clearer picture. When we are thinking, some of our attention is on our thought streams, so we miss what is happening in front of our very eyes. We can't make course corrections which serve us well if we can't recognise opportunities or dangers as and when they occur.

As well as paying attention with our eyes, it makes life so much easier if we pay attention with all our other senses too. Listening for example, is a powerful tool in being aware of all the factors in each interaction and event as it unfolds.

So often we think we are listening, but we are not paying full attention to whomever we are listening to. Most people listen to respond, rather than listening to understand. When someone else is speaking, they start to say something and our mind jumps in with an answer, or something their words remind us of. The mind disagrees before hearing the whole sentence, or agrees, but has to add something to their words before they even finish speaking them.

I was brought up in a house where everyone spoke over each other, so I learnt to do the same.

It was the only way to get a word in edgeways! I had to communicate in this way to be heard at all. But with this way of communicating, I was rarely heard, and I rarely heard what others meant. I only heard my interpretation of their words and I often jumped in before they had finished, so I never got the full picture.

I had an opinion on what I thought they said though. Oh yes, I did indeed! I was triggered into anger by so many things, because I didn't stop for a moment and pay attention, to actually listen and understand what the other person was saying.

When you pay attention and listen without the need to jump in and reply, until there is space to do so, you hear so much more. You hear the doubt and insecurity behind the rudeness, you hear the fear behind the anger, you hear the sadness behind the controlling dialogue. You are much more likely to uncover the true meaning of another's words when you pay full attention to them.

This can also be applied to physical pain. When you pay attention to your body, it speaks to you. You can learn so much, just by listening to your body's signals. When your body has your attention, it doesn't need to create such loud and intense symptoms. Therefore, paying attention not only gives you more clues and insight into what your body needs, it also reduces pain levels and acuteness of symptoms.

It does require practice though, to get effective results. In my experience, it is also much easier and more simple to have someone with prior experience and understanding to guide you through the process.

Someone who knows how to pay attention when the pain is intense, when it feels all consuming.

We are so used to resisting and tensing against painful symptoms, that we struggle to recognise when we are doing this. Another person who has an objective outlook to the pain, can see what you don't see and guide you to recognise where you are fighting against your body.

The closest I can get to being with you in person, is to provide some exercises and tips in part four, which will help you to begin changing your relationship with pain.

Paying attention will be included in these exercises. You can then see more clearly what you are doing, or not doing to contribute towards the level of pain you are currently experiencing.

Patience is also going to be required when using these exercises. In the past I wasn't a very patient person at all. I always wanted results immediately. This can be useful, and it can also be a hindrance.

Being impatient can be useful, in that it will guide you towards the most effective and efficient means to achieving good results, rather than continuing with that which is not effective. But it will also work against good results, because you start trying to force things to happen now. It's much more effective if you are patient and let the results unfold, as you learn to resist less and allow more. Patience, I've discovered, can actually speed up the process of healing.

As I said before, it's a dance. We slip back into old habits; resisting, forcing, and trying to make the pain go away. It does get easier though, especially when you learn to be patient and pay attention to where you are holding on. You will then get to see where you are tensing and struggling against the pain.

Backward steps in a dance are just part of the routine and are not judged to be a problem. Treat this dance with pain in the same way; there's no failure, just another step in the routine. With this approach, the dance will become much lighter and easier.

In time, you will get more practiced at becoming and remaining aware. You will learn to give your body what it needs when it needs something and simply relax and let it do its job of healing when it needs nothing.

One last thing on paying attention. In order to recognise what is actually taking place in your body and the world around you, it is necessary to pay attention and switch your mode of operation from transmit to receive. As you start to practice paying attention, you begin to spot earlier and earlier, when you are focused on transmitting.

Once you recognise you are transmitting, in the form of talking or thinking, you will be able to stop and change to receive mode. In receive mode, you will have access to a whole host of new information and signals, to inform you what needs doing, or not doing, to support your body in its healing process.

Chapter 30
Giving up the why

There is one thing which really holds up the healing process and that is needing to know why.

As soon as we start looking for a reason why something has happened, or is happening, we are hooked into a world of never-ending searching and questioning.

The mind will always come up with possible answers as to why something is happening the way it is. But generally, none of them are satisfactory to the mind, so it takes note of the idea and holds onto it, whilst it continues to search for a better solution. This uses up an inordinate amount of energy and creates a huge amount of tension in the body.

We remain locked into a perpetual downward spiral which is more and more tiring, increasing tension all the while.

Or we can't find a reason and are tortured by the helplessness of it all, stuck in a seemingly locked state with no way out.

Even if we settle on a suitable reason, this can be just as debilitating as never quite finding out why. Thinking we have the answer will keep us stuck in a scenario we believe to be true. It will lead to thinking about it, trying to find a solution. A solution which is often elusive because we are lost in thought and unable to see the possible options available at the time.

Solutions, in my experience, present themselves continually if we are present and able to recognise that they are a solution. I find a solution comes along more readily, when I stop perceiving the situation as wrong or bad, or someone else's fault.

Labelling the situation as bad or wrong will put you in the role of the victim and will keep the mind in play, trying to find out how to make things better for you. Or a self-defeatist attitude may develop, and you will always remain disempowered and unable to address your circumstances.

No-one is ever to blame for your current situation. Not even yourself. This can take a while to realise for sure. But blame will just create an inner battle, which increases tension in your body and reaffirms the rigid thinking patterns. It will also prevent you from seeing a way out of your current situation. Blame serves no purpose and will keep you restricted and blind to possible solutions.

Blame is also a big part of the 'needing to know why' programme. If you can stop blaming yourself or others, you will find life opens up and becomes more gentle and easy.

The mind also wants to find a reason for what has happened, so it can come up with a plan to make sure it won't happen again. This has never worked for me. No matter how many precautions I took to ensure bad things didn't happen, something always went awry, and I became more ill, angrier, or more anxious.

The mind is a limited tool which can be very creative and ingenious, but ultimately keeps you in a holding pattern that is restrictive and dysfunctional.

I propose a different approach...

Stop needing to know why!

Every time you see your mind searching for an answer, stop, pause and let it go. The best way to do this is to turn your focus onto something else. My suggestion would be to learn a technique to become more aware of the still, silent space within. This will give you a solid foundation of awareness to draw on when pain increases, or emotions run amok.

If you don't have a technique yet, decide on a default option you can turn your attention to whenever you notice you are trying to work out why something is the way it is.

Whatever you choose to replace the 'needing to know why' thinking patterns, make sure you apply them each and every time you are caught in them.

I'm always pleasantly surprised when solutions come out of nowhere, without even looking for them. It's like the Universe knows I need help before I do and delivers a solution instantly.

The only thing which holds up this process, is my lack of alertness. If I'm thinking and arguing against what is happening, I miss the solutions in front of me.

Try it and see how it works for you…

Chapter 31
Resistance is futile

I always remember the phrase, 'Resistance is futile' from the Star Trek Voyager series. A species called 'The Borg', who were very powerful, always sent this message when their spaceship locked on a transporter beam to another ship. They were a dominant species made up of Cyborgs and had vastly superior technology. So they were mostly correct - resistance is futile!

It's the same with emotions and physical sensations. Resistance will not make anything any easier. Nor will it make the emotion, or physical sensation go away.

Resistance is in fact the main reason we suffer. This is because resisting intensifies the emotion or physical sensation in the body.

A good analogy I use to understand this process and the effect resistance has on us and our body, is to relate our body to a hosepipe. The water flowing through the pipe represents our emotions. Emotions are energy in motion, e-motion. When we are relaxed and open to this energy passing through us, it's like the water freely flowing through the hosepipe with no obstructions or hindrance of any kind.

However, when we resist this energy flow, it is akin to the hosepipe being squashed, or blocked in some way. A blockage in a hosepipe causes it to bulge and eventually burst. Or, if we had a finger over the opening of the hosepipe, it would spray the water with considerable force. It's difficult, if not impossible, to stop the flow of water altogether and requires real effort to try to do so.

In the same way, we have learnt over the years to tense and resist emotions like anger, sadness, or fear, because it is socially unacceptable in many environments. In some cases, it can even be unacceptable in our home environment.

This has created a population of people who can never relax, because we must be vigilant to the slightest sign of emotional expression and take measures to ensure it does not slip out of us at an inopportune moment.

You can't stop anger without also stopping, or curtailing joy and peace. In controlling our unacceptable emotional reactions, we also close ourselves off to all the good coming our way.

Emotion is simply energy moving through us. There's not really any such thing as negative emotion. We make the distinction because we experience this energy very differently. Our experience is dependent on how relaxed or resistant, open or closed we are in any given moment.

This energy is pure life force flowing through us, energising and enlivening the body and keeping us healthy and alive.

However, because we have been trained to resist certain expressions of emotion, we experience them as unpleasant and uncomfortable.

What we label as negative energy, is simply blocked energy. When energy is blocked, the pressure builds, and the feeling is intensified and uncomfortable to experience. The more we resist and the longer we resist, the greater the build-up of blocked energy.

This continues until some part of the body stops working efficiently. If resistance continues, it will fail, break, or distort in some shape or form.

All this resistance takes a huge amount of energy to sustain. Because this is an unconscious process, we do not often recognise the resistance or even know how we are resisting.

That is, until something bursts, breaks, or causes us pain.

It can be useful to think of it like this. Imagine you are in a swimming pool and you have a beach ball. You push the beach ball under the water, so you can no longer see it above the surface. It takes some effort but it's easy to start with.

As time goes on it becomes more and more difficult to sustain. You begin to tire, but you cannot let the beach ball show on the surface, so you continue to hold it down.

More time passes and your muscles ache, but still you must hold it down out of sight. Nobody must know you are holding the beach ball down either. So not only are you tired and aching, you must also pretend you are fine, as well as keeping the beach ball hidden from others.

You continue holding it down, with a fake smile on your face, pretending all is well. Until at some point your muscles give way and the beach ball bursts up out of the water, splashing yourself and everyone nearby.

You are tired and aching, and now you are ashamed. You don't know how it happened, so you can't prevent it from happening again. Yet you still, after a brief rest, push the beach ball down under the water and go again. This time you are even more determined to keep the beach ball hidden, so society, or your peers will accept you as part of the group.

There comes a point when you are so exhausted from this process your body will no longer comply. Symptoms arise, dysfunction happens, and pain becomes part of your daily life.

Looking at it like this you can see how absurd it is to resist your emotions. Resisting causes so much dysfunction and suffering. And yet it needn't be this way.

Once you understand it's the resistance causing the suffering, you have a chance to change things and learn to operate differently.

The only way to operate without causing suffering, is to come back to a natural state. A natural state requires no effort, no doing of any kind. It's like we are a stretched elastic band. The moment we stop and pay attention, the elastic band snaps back into place.

The next step, after understanding resistance is causing the suffering, is to learn how to recognise where and how you are resisting. If you can't accept this is true, at least hoping it's true works as a good starting point.

It really only makes total sense, once you see the difference and get to experience how relaxed, soft, and gentle allowing actually feels.

There are various different ways to begin learning to allow, and let your body re-balance, heal and work efficiently again.

It takes practice though. And commitment. Persistence is also key. We are so well practised at resisting that it takes some time and determination to keep going. Especially when resistance kicks back in and everything feels difficult, uncomfortable, painful, and hopeless again.

What you resist, persists. So, learning to allow, is crucial to reducing pain and symptoms to a lower level. Life force energy will always persist in trying to flow through us. We cannot stop this process, nor would we want to. Our body needs this energy to process and function in order to keep us healthy and alive.

Resisting will always hinder the natural process of homeostasis. The body will always attempt to heal and re-balance itself. Tension gets in the way of this process. No part of the body will function properly if we hold any tension there.

From my own personal experience, I have realised I hold tension in a lot of different locations in my body. I have also recognised that even though I can relax whilst doing nothing, the minute I begin to carry out a task, whether it is walking around, or sitting down reading or writing, the habit of resisting and tensing initiates again, before I even notice.

The Ascension techniques I use are invaluable in this situation. The techniques are mechanical and so you can carry out your task and gently keep thinking a technique. Thinking the technique automatically releases the habit of tensing so it falls away and the body softens and relaxes by itself. I wouldn't have learnt what I know about pain without these techniques.

You can read how to do something in a book, but unless you learn how to apply the theoretical understanding, you will remain locked into the unconscious patterns, unaware of what is causing the suffering to continue.

The interesting thing about seeing the resistance in yourself, is that it's very easy to change. It is empowering to learn, as a direct experience, you have the power to change what you are experiencing in each and every moment.

Emotional repression is at the heart of making this change. Emotions cloud your perception and make it difficult, if not impossible to see what is truly happening.

Just like a firework, once an emotion has been released, all you need to do is sit back and watch the show. You can't stop a firework once the fuse has been lit. You step back to a safe distance and watch.

A firework display is enjoyable from a distance, but it's noisy and scary up close. If you tried to hold a lit firework in your hand, your hand would be badly damaged.

It's the same with emotions. Trying to stop them once the emotion has begun, is destructive and painful. Yet as scary and difficult as it may seem, if you stop resisting the emotion, take a step back and watch it play out, it instantly becomes more gentle and easy to simply watch.

Just like a firework will burn itself out, an emotion will run its course quite quickly if we allow it to. I once read somewhere that an emotion takes up to 90 seconds to run its course. If you allow the emotion it will eventually pass.

However, if you don't allow the emotion, it will continue in a loop until you manage to repress or suppress it.

If an emotion lasts longer than 90 seconds, that's a sure sign you are resisting it, or recreating it. Recreating it is like lighting another firework and the emotional reaction will begin another loop.

We resist not just out of habit, but also out of fear, or dislike. Say a feeling wells up and it feels unpleasant, we do all we can to avoid, or ignore it.

This is like ignoring a knock at your door. If there is someone who has an important message for you, or wants something, they won't go away until they get you to answer their knock. The longer you ignore them the louder and more frequent the knock will be.

If instead you open the door and let them in, they will deliver their message and leave. It's best though if they are angry (from being ignored) that you don't serve them tea. If you serve them tea, they will hang around. If you don't serve them tea, they will leave much sooner. Be sure to leave the door open as well, so their exit is clear and unblocked.

By serving them tea, I mean interacting with the emotion. Interacting with an emotion is usually in the form of having a conversation in your head about the emotional reaction you are experiencing. This interaction will keep the emotion hanging around for much longer than necessary.

Emotions will always settle down by themselves, if you are willing to let it be there and take no action to get rid of it or tame it in any way.

There will be an exercise to assist you in stepping back from the usual interaction we carry out with our emotions, in part four of this book.

The exercise will guide you through the process of allowing and gaining more clarity on how and when you are resisting. Only when you can see more clearly what you are doing and when you are trying to control your emotional reactions, can you begin to let them play out without interfering.

Nothing can be done until you are clear about when you are resisting or not.

Chapter 32
Accepting help

It is really important you get good at asking for and accepting help.

If you're anything like me, this may be much easier said than done. None-the-less you will need to become accomplished at asking for help, if you have chronic pain, or any condition which leaves you struggling or isolated.

It can be hard to ask for help for most of us, because society has often judged us as weak or abnormal to do so. At times, we have been rejected, mocked, shouted at and ignored, amongst other things. Asking for help has come to be associated with rejection, and it can be a tough habit to overcome.

However, the world is full of people who want to help you and who will even benefit greatly from helping you. It is not a one-way street. If you accept help from someone, you are helping them in return. This is because it is very rewarding to help people. To watch someone relax or benefit in some way, is a fulfilling pastime.

I love helping people! I've always naturally offered help wherever it is needed. But it used to be tiring and, in the end, I ran out of energy to help others and needed to help myself first.

Like the example of the oxygen masks on an airplane. You are directed to put your own mask on first. If you don't, and you try to put it on someone before yourself, you may pass out and be of no use to anyone.

I was so bad at asking for help, I had to be told over and over again I must start doing so. I was barely able to walk and in a lot of pain and yet it was so uncomfortable to even receive help if offered to me, let alone actually ask for help.

My lack of willingness to ask for help, meant I've been given plenty of opportunities where I have been forced into accepting and asking for help. Eventually (I can be a slow learner sometimes!) I began to get more comfortable with asking for help before I was actually in dire need. It took plenty of practice though.

This is why I'm dedicating a whole chapter to this topic. It's only when we stop this self-destructive and limiting pattern, that we can begin to enjoy and benefit from all the opportunities and assistance the world has to offer.

For me it was knowing I was actually helping in return, which allowed me to recognise it's a win-win situation when we ask for help. This obvious fact became apparent one day on my 'Mastery of the Self Course' in Spain. I had already started to accept help through necessity. I had even tentatively asked for help voluntarily a few times.

I had begun to recognise it was in fact arrogant, to go against nature and hide and struggle, rather than ask for help. But still it felt difficult and forced. I was terrified of rejection, punishment, or ridicule.

One day I was resting in bed because I had fallen down some steps and sprained my ankle. I was alone in my room when someone knocked on my door.

I called out to say, "come in" and a lovely, quiet, and gentle lady came in and told me she had been sent to come and visit me. Apparently, she had been instructed to offer service to me, to get her out of her solemn depressed state of mind.

We were both new at this, so it felt a bit odd and awkward at first. We weren't sure what 'offer service' meant and so we just chatted to get to know each other to start with. Then this kind and generous lady offered me a neck and shoulder massage. I gratefully accepted as I was aching all over from being immobile.

We continued to chat as she gently massaged my neck and shoulders, which was lovely by the way! She shared how she was struggling, whilst I listened. When she was done talking, I offered some simple suggestions, based on my recent discoveries on the retreat.

By the end of her visit she was thanking me profusely and we both stopped in our tracks and laughed. We both saw the absolute magic that had just unfolded from our seemingly ordinary interaction.

I felt wonderfully rested and relaxed from the massage and full of gratitude. But it was the other lady's state of being which really surprised both of us. She had gone from gloomy and depressed, to animated, relaxed and cheerful. It was like the difference between night and day. The whole room felt different and we had connected with each other, in a way that few human beings ever do.

This connection happened again and again with many others, until I was eventually persuaded that receiving and asking for help held many more gifts than I would ever have believed possible.

You may have to take my word for it right now. But if you start by receiving help when it is offered and just saying 'thank you' and 'yes please', you will begin to overcome the discomfort and fear of asking for help.

Not only will you increase your self-esteem and make life a lot more simple and easy for yourself. You will also make connections with lovely, kind, and interesting people. On top of that, you will also become a part of the solution for the world. You will serve others in a way you never would have discovered if you had not been willing to receive their help.

It's really only something which makes total sense by doing it.

One step at a time. Begin with receiving help when offered and if it's not offered and you need assistance, ask someone to help you.

If the person says no, then ask someone else. Think of rejection as redirection. The person who says no, simply isn't a good match for your requirements. If a person says yes, but makes it sound like it is an inconvenience to do so, just ignore that and thank them profusely. They may just begin offering help in the future, because it feels good to be thanked.

Being thanked can snap people out of their dysfunctional, defensive, or fearful patterns. Gratitude is the foundation for abundance, ease, and joy.

We can make a big change to our own state of being by receiving and asking for help. Expressing thanks and smiling is a really great mood changer.

The whole dynamic of asking and receiving, then giving gratitude and maybe even some wisdom in return, can open up a whole new world.

We feel better, our relationships improve, and our state of wellbeing and health will benefit too.

Don't believe me?

Well you'll have to try it for yourself. You may be forced into it if you don't!

Be playful and curious about what gifts and unexpected connections may come from the simple act of asking for help.

Chapter 33
Rediscovering the unbroken you

The most common trap we fall into is believing what we want, or need, is outside of ourselves.

This belief is borne out of another belief - the belief in separation. This is the underlying belief of all the other misconceptions we learn to be true.

This belief in separation spawns the core root beliefs that most, if not all of us, have learnt. - 'I am not good enough', 'I am not loveable' and 'there is not enough to go around'.

Being less than others, or better than others, is not possible. There is no hierarchy, other than that which one human being imposes on another.

So many roles and ways of doing things are based on this idea of separation and therefore brings forth the idea that one thing, or person can be better or worse than another.

The belief in separation begins from the disconnection to our source. You may call it God, or the Creator, the Universe, Love, Mother Nature, your Higher Self, or simply a Higher Power.

This disconnection is theoretical only. All belief is only a thought, on repeat in our unconscious mind. A belief is not necessarily true. It is simply a conclusion you once decided was true, based on a past experience.

One of the key things I have learnt, since I began ascending, is it doesn't matter what you believe. The truth will always come out in the end. The one sure way to know what is true, or not true, is to go beyond the theoretical concept to a direct experience.

For example, I could talk to you about chocolate. I could describe what it tastes like and persuade you it's delicious. But you will never know for sure what it is really like, until you taste it and experience it for yourself.

It is exactly the same with presence.

We can understand connecting to and exploring the stillness within will be enjoyable and good for us. However, we can continue to read about what it's like living in the now, experiencing peace and happiness forever, but never actually get to experience it.

And just like with the chocolate, once you have tasted it, you will know it's real and will most likely want more. However, when you haven't actually tasted the chocolate, you only know intellectually what it tastes like, so the impact is minimal.

What makes all the difference in the world is using a technique which takes you within, to a direct experience of peace. A technique that automatically dissolves all the stress in your nervous system, until there is nothing left to take your attention away from the still, silent, peaceful space within.

This still, silent space within is not just a peaceful break from daily strife. It is not only your natural state, it is also who you really are.

We have missed this part of ourselves, because the thoughts, emotions and body sensations take up all of our attention.

As you begin to explore the real 'you' which is the permanent aspect - unmoving and unchanging, still and silent - your life on the outside starts to change.

Sometimes all that needs to change is your perception. Sometimes big changes begin to happen as we get clearer and clearer about what we really want and what really fulfils us. How beautiful that these desires also serve all of humanity at the same time!

Everything we've ever wanted is within and so when we discover this storehouse of hidden gems we can rest. We can really rest, as the outer quest falls away and the inner cosmic exploration begins.

We can be our true self and live life without limitation, which will turn the tables on everything we've believed to be true.

In the light of the truth we experience within, everything else becomes lit up and revealed in its purity.

We no longer have to search for peace, or love, or happiness. We no longer have to struggle and strive and strain to be successful or fulfilled.

Action happens, life goes on as it did before, and we still have desires and preferences. But we are no longer governed by false and limiting beliefs and no longer have to do anything to be loved, or acceptable to others.

Our true self is perfection personified, and all of life will line up to support us, when we are aligned with the inner source of everything that's in existence.

Everything you do happens through you. Everything you say comes through you, without the need to think it over, or deliberate.

You become more efficient and effective at everything you do.

The search is over. You already have what you were looking for. So you can finally get on with the business of living now.

Thank goodness!

Do you believe this is possible?

You may or you may not.

Thankfully you don't have to believe it's true. You just have to be willing to follow your heart and learn how to experience this for yourself.

Then you will know for yourself, that it is actually true. Then you will know for sure, you are in fact what you have been looking for all this time.

YOU are already that which you seek. You are unbroken, whole and complete exactly as you are. When you align with this truth, your body relaxes and heals all by itself.

Which makes life really simple, easy, and much less complicated. Less effort and more enjoyment. Less straining and fighting. More acceptance and grace. Every part of you works better when you allow it to re-calibrate from stillness and silence.

Chapter 34
Equal importance

When you are fully present everything in life is easier.

One of the factors which makes life easier, is you have a more expanded view of the world around you. In this expanded view, you have a much greater awareness of all your surroundings than when you are not present. Not only are you aware of more, you are also aware of everything equally.

This means there is no 'one thing' that captures your attention more than anything else.

When you view and experience everything equally, this means nothing is overwhelming, or intense. This is because overwhelm, or intensity only happens when your attention is narrowed down and focused mostly on one thing. This one thing then becomes or feels huge because it fills your awareness.

It's not that it is actually big, it just feels this way because it has all of your attention.

If you compare the one thing which has all of your attention with a pea, you get a clearer idea of the effect this narrowed down focus has on you.

When something has all of your attention, it may be small, but it is like holding a pea directly in front of your eye. With the pea up close and personal, it is all you will see. There is no perspective. Consequently, whatever the pea represents has all of your attention, so it will feel very uncomfortable, all-encompassing and no other choice will feel possible. This is because you will not be able to see any other options, or information which will give you a clearer picture of the situation.

The pea therefore appears huge and blocks your view of any possible solutions, or factors, that could potentially change the way you experience the pea.

When you are thinking, you maintain this narrowed down, up close view of the pea. The problem is insurmountable.

However, if you stop for a moment and simply pay attention, it has the effect of moving the pea further away from you.

As the pea moves further away, it begins to feel more and more comfortable, as you gain perspective and space grows between you and the pea.

When the pea moves back into its natural place and occupies no more attention than anything else, it could be compared to the pea being on a table on the other side of the room.

With the pea on the other side of the room, it now feels small and easy to see, for what it really is.

Therefore, if the pea is a problem which needs solving, it is now bite sized and much more manageable. Plus, there is a much greater view of the pea's context, providing understanding and a wide range of possible solutions and opportunities to assist you in solving the problem.

It is the same with any problem, person or situation which has all of your attention. Each of these will also, most likely, have a continual internal dialogue playing on repeat in your mind.

If you want to dial down the intensity of emotion and slow down, or even cease the internal dialogue, you will need to pause and pay attention. When you do this, the thing that is bothering you, can shrink back down to its natural size.

This of course includes physical pain. In the context of pain, by simply putting your attention on the body and taking note of where exactly you feel the pain, will begin to change your experience of the pain.

When we resist, or try to ignore pain, it will feel intense. It can often feel like it's a large area that is painful, because your senses are unable to pinpoint the location of the pain, due to confused, conflicting thoughts, or an overload of information. Sometimes it can feel like the pain encompasses your entire body. But as we pause and watch our body, we get more clear signals on the precise location and size of the painful area.

For example, if my right hip is sore, it can appear as if it's the entire hip and top of my leg which is experiencing the physical sensation. When I look again and attentively observe the site of the pain, I get a clearer picture and discover it is in fact emanating out from my hip bone. As I continue to watch this part of my body, the pain is more identifiable as coming from a much smaller area.

I can then allow my attention to expand to more of my body, which has the effect of reducing the intensity.

Alternatively, in observing, my attention is drawn to one, or two, or more parts of my body and the initial painful or sore sensation reduces, as my attention widens.

There will be an exercise in part four, to give you a concise and clear instruction on how to experiment in this way with your own pain and / or body symptoms.

Giving everything equal importance balances out our experience of life, so no one thing dominates your attention.

Your body can then resume the necessary process of healing the part of the body that is damaged or working ineffectively.

When the habit of resistance and tensing is very strong and firmly established, it can take a while to release all stored tension. It can seem difficult to remain relaxed, so the body can continually repair and recover its natural state of functioning.

Gentle persistence is required to retrain the resistance pattern to a more relaxed and rested state. Underlying fear can undermine this process. It can take quite some time, practice, and faith to change this habit into a more natural and nurturing one, which supports a functional and healthy body.

Ongoing guidance and effective techniques are an important part of the retraining process. You will find they are necessary to revert the body back to its original and natural state, where it functions at an optimal level of health.

Part Four

How to make the choice

THE POWER TO CHOOSE

"Choice implies consciousness — a high degree of consciousness. Without it, you have no choice. Choice begins the moment you disidentify from the mind and its conditioned patterns, the moment you become present. Until you reach that point, you are unconscious, spiritually speaking. This means that you are compelled to think, feel, and act in certain ways according to the conditioning of your mind. Nobody chooses dysfunction, conflict, pain. Nobody chooses insanity. They happen because there is not enough presence in you to dissolve the past, not enough light to dispel the darkness. You are not fully here. You have not quite woken up yet. In the meantime, the conditioned mind is running your life. Similarly, if you are one of the many people who have an issue with their parents, if you still harbor resentment about something they did or did not do, then you still believe that they had a choice — that they could have acted differently. It always looks as if people had a choice, but that is an illusion. As long as your mind with its conditioned patterns runs your life, as long as you are your mind, what choice do you have? None. You are not even there. The mind-identified state is severely dysfunctional. It is a form of insanity. Almost everyone is suffering from this illness in varying degrees. The moment you realize this, there can be no more resentment. How can you resent someone's illness? The only appropriate response is compassion. If you are run by your mind, although you have no choice you will still suffer the consequences of your unconsciousness, and you will create further suffering. You will bear the burden of fear, conflict, problems, and pain. The suffering thus created will eventually force you out of your unconscious state."

- Eckhart Tolle -

Chapter 35
The right attitude

Learning how to make the choice for peace begins with having the right attitude. An attitude which cultivates an effective approach and changes your habitual patterns of fighting and resistance, to one of ease and grace.

An attitude is the way we look at and view ourselves and the world. The attitude we adopt, is either one based on the past, or one that is clear of all restrictions and free to approach life with fresh innocence in <u>this</u> moment.

Cultivating the right attitude is key to any practice, any new project, any new thing you decide to do. Intent is a big part of what impact your new approach will have.

We have learnt to approach life in a very set and limited way. In order to change your approach, to gain the greatest impact from a new practice or technique, you must first set your intent.

The intent can be a focus for you to return to again and again, until it becomes second nature and your approach is naturally aligned with what you intend.

The core aspects of your intent can be anything you want them to be. Gently reinforcing intent by repetition, with an openness and willingness to fully commit to a new practice, gives you the best chance of changing the habitual patterns and sustaining the new habit. It is a beneficial and easy approach to maintain.

Choosing an approach that is natural and easy, is key to being able to sustain and maintain anything. If you are open and willing to try anything, you will have less resistance and more ease in anything you attempt to do.

As well as being open and willing, innocence plays a vital role in keeping your approach simple and easy. It can be simple to set the intent and be innocent at the beginning, but as time goes on innocence can quickly fall away, as we fall back into the habitual pattern of struggle and strain.

Always wipe the slate clean after each time you do an exercise or practice any technique in this book. Don't compare one session to another, ever. Your subjective experience is going to change from one moment to the next. As stress releases, the state of your mind and body is going to be different moment by moment.

Innocence allows you to be present with what your experience is like right now, with no judgement of it being not good enough or wrong, or failing, or bad. With innocence comes surrender to 'what is', so 'what is' can move and change, as your whole system recalibrates, coming back to its natural state effortlessly and easily.

Nike has a great slogan to adopt in this situation - 'Just do it'.

When we 'just do it', when we follow the instruction and apply it to the practice, results will follow. The mind will always have an opinion on how well your practice is going. Your own job is to not listen and just do it.

It can take a while to get used to no longer following your existing thought patterns. We have trained for many years and followed the activity in our minds, believing it is who we are. The recognition of who we really are - that which is aware of thought - can take time to sink in and feel true.

The best advice I remember and now give, is to commit to a new practice for a period of 6 weeks. By doing this it provides a time frame for the results to be revealed.

As all these exercises and techniques have an accumulative effect, it is helpful to 'just do it' for 6 weeks and then and only then, assess how you are doing. This way you will see the results clearly and be more motivated to continue.

If you try to assess how you are doing at the beginning, you will be confused, or even put off and decide it is not working, or not worth it. As the stress moves, it can be disorientating and disturbing. We've learnt to resist a lot of emotional responses, and resistance always intensifies the sensations and causes suffering.

In order to transcend the discomfort of the feeling and sensations of stress moving, we need to keep going and push past the resistance to break through the habit. This enables us to experience life without as much resistance and struggle.

Yes, this is possible, and it is easy to do, with effective techniques and ongoing guidance. Ongoing guidance is crucial to moving past old patterns. Otherwise, we get lost in the stress releasing and cannot return to the simplicity of the instruction and actually apply it, without the intellect getting involved.

So, to recap ....

- Be open and willing

- Return to Innocence again and again

- Commit to 6 weeks

- Ask for help and guidance

Then the process will be much more simple, easy, enjoyable and effective.

Chapter 36
Feel the body

This exercise is very simple and easy to practice. You don't need to sit or lie in any particular position. It is helpful however, to find somewhere quiet to practice it to begin with.

Sit or lie in a comfortable position. Prop yourself up with cushions, put your feet up or keep them on the ground. Find the position most comfortable for you, which allows you to feel supported, so you will be able to relax most easily.

Close your eyes and give yourself permission to relax.

As you close your eyes, do so gently. Allow your eyelids to slowly and easily float down and cover your eyes. Make sure you do not tightly squeeze your eyes to keep them closed. Gently let your eyes remain softly closed and relaxed for the rest of the exercise.

Now allow yourself to be in your body. Become aware of your entire body and tune into it, as if it is a radio station.

Ask yourself - ' What do I feel and where do I feel it? '

Then just simply pay attention to your body and watch.

Notice what sensations you can feel and observe them as if you are conducting an experiment, to which you do not know the outcome.

Note what you are feeling and where, and continue to watch that part of the body, as if you are watching a movie, or television programme.

Have no opinion about what you are observing, just gently watch and see what happens next.

If your mind wants to analyse what you are noticing … stop … pause … and bring 100% of your attention back on to that part of your body … gently pay full attention and continue to watch it. If your mind wanders off into thought again, simply stop … pause … and again bring 100% of your attention back onto that part of your body. Any time your mind wanders off into thought again simply rinse and repeat the - stop … pause … 100% attention back on to the body instruction.

Now, have the intention to allow.

Allow that part of your body to soften and relax. Allow that part of your body to come back to life. Allow that part of your body to resume all-natural movement. Allow the blood flow and oxygen to reach all of this part of your body. Allow any tension to dissipate and healing to happen. Allow whatever movement that wants to happen, to happen.

Feel this part of your body fully.

Appreciate what this part of your body is for.

Express gratitude for this part of your body.

Love this part of your body fully.

And watch …

Observe and see if anything changes while you just watch and allow … watch and allow.

Does movement begin to happen in this part of your body?

Does it begin to soften and relax?

Does anything change as you watch? What do you notice? Anything? Nothing? There is no correct answer, or way of doing this exercise. Watch your body, see what you notice, allow movement, and just continue to watch.

There is nothing to do, nowhere to go.

Just watch.

You cannot get this exercise wrong. Nor can you get it right. You just watch and allow ... watch and allow.

If a sigh comes, let it come. If a deep breath happens, let it happen. If your tummy gurgles, let it gurgle. If you want to stretch your body, stretch your body. If you feel like crying, cry. If words come, speak them out loud with no need to understand or edit, just speak them softly. Or if you want to shout and swear just do it, if you are alone and free to do so.

If you feel sad, feel sad. If you feel angry, feel angry. If you feel happy, feel happy. If you want to laugh out loud, laugh out loud.

Whatever you feel, let yourself feel it. Feel it 100 % and it will move.

And then just watch. Watch and allow ... watch and allow. Watch whatever happens and just let it happen. Naturally and easily.

Allow the body to unravel and release all tension. Allow your body to twitch and adjust if it needs to. Notice what happens and let it happen. If nothing happens, great ... just watch. Watch and allow ... watch and allow. Always gently, always easily.

Then allow your awareness to expand to include the rest of your body. Is there anywhere else that catches your attention?

Allow your attention to go to any part of your body you become aware of. What else do you notice?

And just watch. Let your attention move around your body to wherever it wants to go.

Are there other areas of your body that grab your attention?

Watch and be curious. With your awareness, feel your way around your body. Become familiar with every single part of your body.

And.... just.... watch.

Now become aware of your body as a whole being. Be aware of all of your body at once. Expand your awareness to include every single part of you. Every single cell. And ... just ... rest.

When you are ready, take 3 deep breaths slowly and gently. Then rest for a few moments.

In your own time, open your eyes slowly and gently.

Allow your awareness to take in your surroundings. Notice what is there around you in the room you are in.

Give yourself a moment to just rest.

Then when you feel ready, continue with your day, bringing this new level of calm with you as you go about your day.

. . .

Here is a brief recap for you to refer to, once you have read the full instructions:

1. Sit or lie in a comfortable position in a quiet place.

2. Gently close your eyes.

3. Tune in to your body.

4. Watch your body.

5. Pay attention to the area that hurts.

6. Watch and allow ... watch and allow.

7. Allow movement and healing to take place.

8. Watch and allow ... watch and allow.

9. Appreciate your body, give it gratitude, give it love.

10. Continue to watch and allow.

11. Expand the awareness to other parts of your body.

12. Watch and see where your attention goes.

13. Become aware of all of your body.

14. Take three deep breaths.

15. Open your eyes and take in your surroundings.

16. Pause ... take a moment, then bring this calm into your day.

. . .

If at any time it is still quite painful, just watch.

However, if the pain intensifies and doesn't abate, stop ... pause ... and breathe for a moment. Let the intensity subside. Intensity increases when there is resistance to the movement.

You cannot force yourself to relax. You cannot make yourself allow what is happening. Allowing occurs when you stop resisting.

If everything feels tense, rigid, locked and nothing is softening or relaxing, simply acknowledge it. Acknowledge the sensation you feel and let it be okay. Let it be okay that it is not okay. Don't try to change how you feel.

Acknowledge that you are doing your best. You are not failing if it does not feel easier.

This is important.

It's important to understand you are not doing anything wrong if this exercise does not bring you immediate relief.

You are not doing anything wrong if this exercise increases the pain.

Just let it be exactly how it is right now. Let it hurt. Stop fighting the pain. Take the label of 'pain' away and just pay attention to that part of your body. Where is the sensation emanating from? Is there a centre to the sensation? Does your body need anything right now? If it does, do whatever needs to be done.

If nothing presents itself to be done … just watch.

Let yourself just be for a moment and give yourself a break. This can be hard and you are incredibly brave and resourceful for doing it. To go through life in chronic pain is tough. I know how that feels, I lived through the feeling of isolation and agony for many years.

So be gentle with yourself and if this exercise just makes things worse, stop and try one of the other exercises in this part of the book.

You may wish to read through the exercise a few times to familiarise yourself with the instructions. Then close your eyes and explore. You may also wish to read through the instructions each time, just before you use the exercise, until you become more familiar with them.

Do the same for the following exercises too.

Chapter 37
Loosen up

There came a point when I recognised how tightly I was holding my body. The tension in some areas was very intense and locked in. There was a rigidity in my body that became so apparent, I wondered why I had never noticed it before.

Trying to relax would sometimes cause the pain to become more intense. There was a forcefulness I seemed unable to counteract.

My son had a profound experience one night where, as he described it, everything became loose. He said it was really lovely and he had never felt so calm and relaxed before. I recognised he had become present and surrendered all his stress in that moment, as he was listening to music.

This exercise is a product of the experience my son had. I played with it for a while myself and got to see how tight some parts of my body could still be even though there was no pain. I suggested it to others who were still in pain and it was very useful to all who tried it.

The body, as I've said before, responds to all the thoughts we have. So, I capitalised on that and created an exercise which gives instructions to loosen up and allow the body to unwind and re-balance itself.

As with all the exercises in part four, it is an eyes closed method which is most beneficial if you find somewhere quiet and comfortable, where you are well-supported.

With your eyes gently closed, take a moment to settle down and become aware. Notice the chair, bed, or floor underneath you and just gently observe the sensations you are aware of.

Give yourself full permission to rest now. Take a deep breath and let it go, then observe what happens next for a moment or two.

Tune into your body and allow every part to loosen up just a little bit. Then a little bit more, looser, and looser.

Imagine your body is unwinding slowly and easily. Becoming more soft, more pliable, more gentle.

Let this process continue as you allow every part of your body to become looser and looser, softer and softer. Relaxed and more relaxed.

Unwinding, little bit by little bit. Unravelling more and more, easily and gently, softening and relaxing.

Become the witness to this unravelling and unwinding. Watch the body as if you are an alien from outer space, curious as to what you are watching.

Letting it happen slowly and gently. No forcing or trying. Just gently observing as your body loosens up, softens and relaxes more and more fully, gently and easily.

How loose can you become?

Continue to allow the body to soften and relax. Allow it to become even more loose and fluid. Allow all movement to happen as your body becomes more harmonious and graceful.

Give yourself a few minutes to allow the body to unwind and soften. Just relax and enjoy the sensations. Observe it all, without any need for any particular result. Just notice what is happening and watch it all from a neutral standpoint.

After a few minutes of allowing the loosening up to continue, just rest for a while and observe what the experience feels like. Notice all sensations in the body and just watch them.

Become aware of the space around your body, and when you feel ready open your eyes slowly and easily.

Stay rested and gently observe your surroundings. Take it all in with curiosity. Be attentive and aware with no opinion of what you see. Just notice what is there and observe.

Again, tune into your body and allow it to become a little more loose. Allow your body to soften and relax a little more.

If you meditate, you could now close your eyes and begin meditating with whatever technique you use.

When you decide to get up, do so slowly and deliberately. Think about where you place your hands and how you will move into standing.

Allow every movement to be slow, gentle and smooth.

Before you begin to walk and carry out daily tasks, allow your body to loosen up again and soften.

If you notice your body has become tense again, simply allow it to soften and loosen for a moment before you continue on with what you are doing. If pain captures your attention, or becomes more intense, again allow your body to soften and relax a little bit and loosen up.

You can keep on applying this as you go about your day and see what difference it makes to your experience of your body and the movement it makes.

The intent is enough if part of you still feels locked. Don't force anything, just work within the parameters your body is comfortable with for now. Explore this exercise for a few days to a week and see what happens.

Baby steps are okay. Whatever you experience is okay.

The holding in patterns we have had for a long time will likely keep re-establishing. Be playful and curious and keep applying the instruction to loosen up, soften and unwind the tension held in your body.

Use this exercise with your eyes closed at least once a day, so you can explore what is possible more deeply. The eyes closed practice, along with the support of playing with it eyes open as you move about your day, will allow you to become more present to the holding in pattern.

The more present you become, the more awareness you will have of any tension and your body will begin to relax by itself.

Only when you are aware of what you are doing, can you make another choice and establish a new way of being.

This greater level of awareness from allowing your body to loosen will also have an impact on your mental and emotional state.

It always amazes me how much more I get done when I slow everything down. My mind doesn't understand this at all!

But the proof is in the experience and when the body moves more fluidly and easily, it is more efficient and effective in everything it does.

The other bonus is you feel much more content, and pain will most likely ease or even fade away.

Just be gentle, curious, and open to the possibility of it being different for you in each and every moment.

Chapter 38
Body rhythm

The body knows what to do to remain healthy. We just have to let go and allow it to operate naturally, without interrupting its natural rhythm and flow.

This exercise is useful for tuning back into the body's natural rhythm and becoming more accepting of 'what is'. This allows the current state of your body space to change and re-balance.

Find somewhere quiet and comfortable and settle down to rest. Close your eyes and just simply pay attention for a moment. What is it like to sit or lie there with your eyes closed? Just notice, watch and allow everything to be exactly as it is in this moment.

Then draw your attention into your body and pay attention to what you are aware of happening.

As before, be curious about what you will discover. Become gently attentive to the movement of the internal workings of your body. What do you notice? Just gently observe your body and every movement that is happening within.

Pay attention to the breath as your body breathes in and out. Notice the air flowing in and out. What does that feel like? Where is the movement? Don't concern yourself with how you are breathing, that will come in a later chapter. For now, just observe and become gently attentive to what you observe.

Now draw your attention to your heartbeat. Can you hear it, feel it? Pay attention to the sound, vibration, and any sensations you become aware of. Watch and allow your body to do what it naturally wants to do. Become fully attentive to the rhythm of your heart and just observe it for a moment or two. Feel the movement and go with it. Like you're going with the flow of a river.

Now notice what else is happening in your body. What else is moving and pulsing? Pay attention for a moment and watch, allowing all internal movement to be smooth and gentle and easy.

Maybe your stomach gurgles, just watch and allow.

Maybe your jaw relaxes, just watch and allow.

Maybe your leg or arm moves or twitches, just watch and allow.

See what you notice and just observe it and allow it all to play out in natural harmony and grace.

As you continue to observe the natural rhythm of your body, begin to become aware of the part of your experience that is unmoving, unchanging.

Underlying all the movement, is the context of stillness.

Without straining to notice stillness, just gently pay attention and see if you notice that which does not move. Simply watch the stillest part of your experience and be curious.

You needn't search for the still part, just simply allow it to be revealed to you. More and more fully.

Just rest there for a moment or two and observe, allowing everything to be exactly as it is right now. You can't get this wrong or even right. Whatever you are aware of is perfect.

Just watch whatever you are noticing and let this moment be enough, just as it is.

When you have rested for a while, gently and slowly allow yourself to become more alert. In your own time, open your eyes and blink a few times. Notice your surroundings and allow the information and light rays to come to you as you stay rested in your experience.

Let this moment be enough.

When you feel ready, gently get up and continue on with your day.

As you move about, intend to be aware of your body's natural rhythms and allow your body to breathe and move as it wants to.

At no time do you need to force anything. If you feel strained or tense, or in pain, pause for a moment and allow your natural rhythm to reassert itself. Then gently engage your daily activity from this natural state of harmony and grace.

Chapter 39
Alert listening

Listening is one of the best ways to pay attention more fully. This is because it allows our awareness to soften and widen. Listening to the sounds in our environment will increase our level of alertness and attentiveness. The more alert and attentive we are, the more present we are.

The more present we are, the more pure and clear our experience is. In the purity of experience with no dialogue passing through our mind, pain fades away and only sensations in the body are left which are no longer what you would class as painful.

So, listening can be very useful in the process of changing your relationship with pain.

Again, find somewhere quiet and comfortable and close your eyes. Give yourself permission to rest now. Allow every part of your body to soften and relax, whilst you just watch the space in front of you.

What do you notice right now? Note what you notice with no opinion and no need to change it. Then begin to explore further.

What else do you notice? Pay attention and continue exploring... What else, and... what else? Keep observing and exploring what else you are aware of.

Then begin to listen attentively. What do you hear? What else is there? Keep listening, giving more and more attention to what else there may be in your experience now.

Listen as if you were listening to an orchestra and new sounds keep being played. Listen to the sounds as if the Universe is playing a symphony just for you.

Allow yourself to be enthralled and fully attentive to everything you hear or don't hear.

As you listen, begin to become aware of the silence underlying the sounds you hear. Switch your focus from the content of sound to the context of silence.

Don't strain or search for silence. Just notice the quiet part of your experience now. Listen to the sound of silence.

Again, be curious. What is it like to experience silence? Listen and be fully attentive to silence. Just like on a radio, you can tune into a radio station and hear music. Now you are tuning into radio silence.

Gently attentive, exploring, resting, allowing the silence to be revealed more and more fully.

At this stage you can begin your usual meditation practice if you have one.

After a few minutes of resting and exploring the silence, gently and in your own time slowly open your eyes.

As you open your eyes, take your time, and observe your surroundings, whilst staying rested. Listen again to any sounds you hear in your environment. Listen and pay attention to what you hear with 100% of your attention.

When you feel ready, get up slowly and purposefully. Then engage your day with gentleness and calm.

Listening with 100% of your attention is a wonderful thing to practice as you go about your day. Especially when you are engaging in conversation with someone. Even if they are rude or dominate the conversation or keep talking over you. In fact, it can make a big change to the dynamic if you listen to them attentively, (as if they are important). Be interested in what the other person has to say, not to respond, just to simply understand where they are coming from.

When I started playing with listening more fully in conversation, I started noticing so much more about the other person. I became aware of more than just the words they were speaking. I noticed their body language, their emotional state and the feeling generated from their words became more gentle.

Listening changed my own state too. I became more relaxed, my body softened and the air around us became more alive somehow.

Another very curious thing began to happen in my interactions with other people as a result. The other person would finish what they were saying much sooner and make space for me to speak. They would also seem more interested in what I had to say and would listen to me more fully in return.

I also noticed that my relationship with pain changed too as I listened more and more fully to another person speaking. I stopped being so aware of my body aches and sensations.

All my attention was on the other person. Which filled my awareness, so there was no room for any attention to be on my own thoughts, emotions, or body sensations.

Using this exercise with eyes closed is a great way to begin a meditation session. In my experience, listening cultivates alertness and makes my Ascension practice more pleasant and effective.

Chapter 40
Surrender to the flow

This exercise is designed to facilitate surrender to the natural flow of your body. The inner workings of your body are complex, yet intuitive and intelligent. Your body knows what to do to stay healthy. The only trouble is the mind thinks it knows better!

Every thought passing through your mind has an impact on your body. Each thought is an instruction to the body, and it can get very confusing and debilitating for the body to try and keep up with all the contradictory instructions.

The body is therefore mostly in a holding state by the time you are a young adult. The body is a servant to the mind and will follow each and every instruction it is given as closely as it can.

This holding state of tension and angst is detrimental to your health and the natural flow of bodily operations.

The instructions your thoughts provide are mostly unconscious, therefore it is difficult, if not downright impossible to change them.

So instead this exercise will counteract the instructions without needing to know what they are.

. . .

Make yourself comfortable in a sitting or lying down position, well-supported with cushions or pillows, and in a quiet place where you won't be interrupted.

Gently close your eyes and settle down to rest. Notice the sensation of the support underneath your body and let yourself relax more fully into that support.

Now tune into your body and observe whatever you notice without effort or any need to change what you see or feel. Let yourself relax a little bit more and pay full attention to your body.

Then ask yourself 'where can I do less'?

A little less tension, a little less straining, a little less holding in.

Let yourself go as fully as you can into the moment and let yourself surrender to your body's natural flow. Your body's natural tendency is to heal. Give permission for your body to do whatever it needs to do to heal and operate efficiently.

Again ask 'where can I do less? Then watch and see what you notice and allow every movement that wants to happen, to happen naturally.

Pay attention to your body and notice if you are resisting something. Are you preventing movement and the flow of your body's natural functions? See where you can do less, and relax even more deeply allowing the process of healing to occur.

Keep checking in every now and then with the intent to notice where you can do less, and allow the body to respond and relax more deeply.

If pain arises or existing pain intensifies, do your best to let the feeling of pain flow. Allow it to be there so it can move. Again, give your permission for that part of your body to do less and allow healing to happen. Surrender to the flow, surrender to the body's natural tendency to heal.

Intend to be a little more gentle and allow your body to soften and relax into the flow of healing movement more and more fully.

Be even more gentle, allow and watch whatever is happening in your experience right now. Become the witness to the movement of your body. Have a hands-off approach and let whatever happens happen.

Introduce innocence, with no expectation of what will happen next. Again, see where you can do less. Allow, allow, allow.

Rest for a while longer, for as long as you wish. Then when you feel ready, open your eyes and pay attention to your surroundings.

Notice what you see, hear and smell. Notice what you feel. Notice the support underneath you.

Notice the space around you. Before you stand up ask yourself where can I do less in this next movement? Slowly bring yourself to standing gently, smoothly, and easily.

Again, before you begin walking, intend to do less and move slowly and smoothly as you go about your day.

Chapter 41
Into space

Our body is 99.99% empty space. I remember learning this in a physics lesson when I was only about 14 or 15 years old. My mind could not comprehend this information as my body felt so solid. The same was apparently true for the desk I was sitting at and the chair I was sitting on. I also learnt the molecules vibrate at different rates to give the appearance and feel of something solid.

I have since concluded a painful body part is therefore not as rigid and immovable as it appears to be. A little like a bicycle wheel. When it spins, it acts like a solid object and your hand will bounce off it. Yet if the wheel is still, your hand will easily pass through the gap in-between the spokes.

With this information we can approach our body in a different way, especially when it feels locked into a painful state.

This exercise will naturally draw your attention from the content of particles, to the space within you and thus allow your experience to be more open and allowing.

. . .

As for all the other exercises, find a quiet space where you can be comfortable, either sitting or lying down. Once you are comfortable, gently close your eyes and settle down to rest. Give yourself permission to rest more and more fully. Allow every part of your body to soften and relax, almost melting into the chair or surface you are lying on.

For a moment just watch and see what you notice. There is nothing to do and nowhere to go right now … so just rest and allow whatever happens to happen, while you just observe it all.

Now gently tune into your body and notice what it feels like.

Pay attention to all sensations and just watch them happen, without any need to change what you are noticing.

Feel every part of your body and become fully present and aware of your whole body. Keep watching and allowing whatever happens to happen.

Now take a deep breath and relax even more fully. Gently intend to become aware of the space between the cells in your body. Observe whatever you notice and continue to be aware of the space in between all your body's cells.

Rest there for a moment.

Then gently intend to become aware of the space in the cells of your body. Don't try to do this or strain for a particular experience. Just rest and watch the space that you are aware of.

Continue to gently rest and watch for a while and always allow everything you notice to come and go with no need to control any part of your experience. Just watch and allow, watch and allow.

Rest for as long as you want and then in your own time open your eyes and take in your surroundings. Slowly and gently get up when you are ready to continue on with your day.

. . .

You can also play with this exercise in a different way with your eyes open, as you walk around and carry out your daily tasks. Simply shift your focus from your body and the objects in your surroundings, onto the space around you whenever you remember.

If pain arises or intensifies, simply become aware of the space around you. You can extend this to include awareness of the space in your body as well. Allow any movement your body wants to make in response to this shift of attention.

Be light and playful with your approach to this exercise.

Chapter 42
Appreciation and gratitude

Appreciation and gratitude are very powerful ways of changing the way we think and feel about our body. It changes the dynamic from one of stress, tension, and criticism to a more relaxed, gentle, and calm one.

We rarely give our bodies thanks or appreciation for all they do to keep us alive and interacting with the world around us. In fact, we often take them for granted or complain and judge them as not good enough.

Appreciation and gratitude open us up to a more expansive experience. Appreciation encourages and allows you to flourish in everything you do. Gratitude is the foundation for abundance. It beams out a signal of all you have in your life that is good and acts like a magnet to draw more of this good into your life.

Both appreciation and gratitude cultivate a state which is light, flexible and gentle.

This exercise will have an accumulative impact on your physical health and emotional well-being. It needn't take very long, 5-10 minutes at most.

I suggest you do it once a day, possibly in the morning to set you up for the day, or whenever fits in best with your daily schedule.

. . .

Let's begin … Sit or lie down and get yourself comfortable, then gently close your eyes.

Beginning with the top of your head, simply praise and thank every part of your body, one bit at a time. Slowly, gently, and easily.

Tune in to each body part and say I appreciate all you do for me, thank you. You can be more specific if you like. For example: Thank your hands for enabling me to pick things up and move them around.

If you can't think of anything specific to say, then just a simple I appreciate you, thank you, is perfect.

If the body part you are thanking isn't working well, or is very painful, thank it and appreciate it for doing its best. Or appreciate and thank it for a time when it was working efficiently and freely. You could also imagine it working well again, pain free in the future. Be playful and explore what it would feel like if you could move freely and easily. Imagine the lightness and comfort in your body, like when you were a young child, curious and carefree.

Once you have thanked and appreciated every part of your body, stay resting for a moment and take it all in. Then when you are ready, slowly, and gently get up and ease back into movement and continue on with your day.

. . .

Another way to approach this exercise for when you have less time, is to appreciate your entire body for a moment or two. Then shift the focus and be grateful for your entire body for a few moments longer.... Then continue with the task in hand.

If you find you are criticising part of your body or feeling frustrated with the aches or pain you are experiencing, simply switch over to appreciating and being grateful.

You can change this habit more quickly, if, for every 1 thing you criticise or judge about your body, you find 3 things to appreciate and thank your body for.

Be creative and be willing to allow your body to be different in each and every moment going forward.

Chapter 43
Let your body be your guide

Your body has an innate intelligence programmed into every cell. It knows how to heal everything and requires very little assistance to do so.

In fact, your body will give signals, for anything it needs at any given moment. The only problem is, most of us have forgotten how to listen to our body's, often very clear signals.

In the noise, clamour and busyness of everyday life, your body's requests and requirements get lost amidst all the activity.

In order to get in touch with your body again and become able to discern what it requires; you will need to become quiet and tune in to the body's signalling system.

The last few chapters had several exercises to relax and reset the body-mind system. These exercises are a really useful and beneficial place to begin tuning into the body.

But we spend most of our day with our eyes open and engaged in activity, so it's also important to begin to become more aware of your body's signals whilst carrying out daily tasks.

Another advantage to being much more aware, is you will naturally relax and become more flexible and fluid in all your muscles. This will, in turn, allow movement to become more graceful and easy, using less effort to walk, bend or lift.

In my own experience I had to learn to slow down and stop more frequently to rest and recover. I used to keep going until a job was completed and often felt faint or dizzy, because I ignored my body's signal to pause for a moment and rest.

I was also quite disdainful (I'm ashamed to admit) of people who kept stopping to rest and took (in my opinion) too long completing each task.

It was almost a sense of pride that I could get so much done, in a short space of time. Well it backfired, because it was not sustainable, and my body eventually broke down.

So now I pay more attention to my body and pause to rest whenever I need to. It's important to be flexible and willing to stop before you reach a suitable milestone in your activity. Some days I don't need much rest and other days I need to stop more often.

One reason I need to stop more often, is when I'm engrossed in an activity, my poor postural habits or tendency to tense certain areas of my body, become exacerbated.

For example, right now as I'm writing this chapter, I became aware I was clenching my jaw and bending forward. Both are very strong habits that initiate again and again when I am focused on a task. I also strain my eyes and they frequently become sore and dry from lack of blinking, because I tend to stare when I am concentrating.

The first step then, is simply to intend to pay attention and become more aware. The intention alone will increase your ability to remember and will also increase your level of alertness. Increased alertness gives you a much clearer picture of what your body is doing from moment to moment.

Being gentle with yourself is of utmost importance as well. Poor posture and holding tension in our body is a very common and strong habit which has been reinforced over many years. You will forget again and again, so be gentle and patient to the best of your ability. Gentleness also relaxes your body and increases alertness, so it's a very useful approach to apply.

I've noticed almost everyone is, to varying degrees, hunched at the shoulders. Not only that, but it's happening from an increasingly younger and younger age.

It's like we are all carrying the weight of the world on our shoulders. It's common, but it's not natural and like any habit that we've learnt, it can be undone.

Put another way, we can retrain ourselves to cultivate a new habit.

It can seem daunting to attempt to introduce a new habit, when the existing habit seems so set in stone. But our bodies are like an elastic band that we've stretched and held out of shape.

When we learn to relax and begin a consistent schedule of relaxation sessions, there is a possibility the body will be able to ease back into place again. Just like an elastic band, if we can let go of the tension holding us out of shape, the body has the opportunity to come back to its natural posture. Sometimes the body needs a little assistance to re-establish its original shape, but relaxation is an important first step.

Then all we need to do is rinse and repeat until we learn to remain in a relaxed state. All it takes is a greater level of alertness, so we quickly recognise when we are tensing or clenching unnecessarily.

Slowing down and becoming more deliberate with our movement, can really make a big difference too. So often I have suddenly noticed I'm rushing to get somewhere or finish a task, to move on to the next one on a very long 'to-do' list.

Taking the approach of one job at a time, has resulted in more attention on each job. Which means the job gets completed sooner, with less tension and more ease. This is obviously more efficient!

I'm also much more effective when 100% of my attention is only on one job. Not to mention more present and therefore more content, which makes each job more enjoyable.

I'm not even sure why I used to rush about at top speed everywhere.

It was a habit that crept in for no apparent reason. It may have been I thought I would get more done if I rushed through my day. However, since I have become more aware and have slowed down, I actually get more done. Partly because I don't make so many mistakes, or have to repeat my actions to get the desired result.

I'm reminded of the proverbial story of the tortoise and the hare. I used to think it was nonsense and if the hare hadn't sat down to rest, he would have reached the finish line first. But in practice, the rushing around trips you up, tires you out and makes for a very stressful life.

Plus, when you rush, the habits pile up and up, until your body is bent out of shape and starts to become more and more painful.

Another thing a large majority of people forget to do is stay hydrated. When we become dehydrated, the body does not work as efficiently.

You may already know this, but if you don't, sorry to be the bearer of bad news. Caffeine and alcohol dehydrate us. Any drink with caffeine or alcohol will likely cancel out any of the benefits of drinking fluid.

A glass of water on the other hand is the best way to rehydrate and assist the body in all its natural functions. Isn't that right mum?!

Apparently, (I don't know if this is true or not!) When we feel hungry, it's often because we are in fact thirsty.

When I put on weight at the beginning of menopause, I applied this theory. I drank a glass of water instead of eating, to slow down my weight gain. I felt better for it, but I'm not sure if it made a difference to my weight.

However, I did stop to drink a glass of water, which meant it killed two birds with one stone. I like efficiency!

So, to recap:

1. Intend to pay more attention and become more alert and aware.

2. Slow down and be more deliberate with every movement.

3. Rest when needed, which may be more often on some days than others.

4 Allow your body to find its own rhythm and pace.

5. Give your body what it needs e.g. water; food; fresh air; exercise

When you begin paying more attention, pain may become more evident. There is a Rumi quote which I have found quite useful.

"These pains you feel are messengers, listen to them".

It's a 'do exactly what it says on the tin' kind of instruction.

Listen to your body. Listen to understand. Listen and be willing to do something differently, so your body can manage to heal and adjust to the strains of everyday living.

If pain is intensifying or at an uncomfortable level, stop for a moment. Tune in to your body and pay attention. Feel the aliveness permeating every cell. Take a few deep breaths into your belly. And listen, really listen to your body. Ask "what does my body need right now?"

Then wait for the answer.

If you become really quiet and still, the answer will come.

Learn to listen well and listen often. Then answer your body's requests with love and compassion.

To help you with listening to your body, here is a short exercise to give you an idea of how to approach being more alert and aware. It will help you to notice more quickly what your body needs, at the same time as taking the pressure off it, from the accumulated habits which have built up over time.

. . .

Moving with awareness exercise

You can use this exercise with your eyes open as you are completing your usual daily tasks.

At any point in your day, no matter what you are doing, simply pause for a moment and take stock of what your body is feeling right now.

Grounding is important, so notice where your feet are in contact with the ground. Bring all of your attention onto your body and notice how it feels. Notice the breath flow in and out. Notice your heartbeat and notice the aliveness in every cell in your body.

Then get ready to continue to carry out the movement or task you were in the middle of. As you continue, do so slowly and deliberately. Let your body find it's centre of balance and allow the movement to flow through you.

Let the movement be gentle and easy as you pay attention to how your body is moving and see if you can make the movement even more gentle and graceful.

Check to see if your body wants to move slightly differently in order to be more gentle and graceful. How does that feel? Natural, easy? Or awkward and unfamiliar? Both are perfectly fine. Just go with it and see how the movement unfolds as you continue to complete your task.

As you walk, intend to connect with the ground and allow your body to be fully present. Are you fully 'in' your body?

If not, come back to putting more attention on your whole body. If you are doing something with your hands, bring your focus of attention onto your hands and be 100% attentive to what they are doing. Be curious about how they are moving to carry out the task. Notice the sensations in your fingers as they move. Notice where they are in contact with the objects you are touching.

I'm playing with this right now as I type these words, so I'll share with you what I'm noticing as I type. Firstly, I feel the sensation of the keys as I touch them. I am more aware of the movement of each finger as they move from one key to the next.

I become more present naturally as I observe what I am doing. Then my spine lengthens, and my shoulders drop by themselves as I notice they are a bit hunched. Everything becomes much more still and quiet. I am more aware of the sound the keys are making as I press them down.

I'm not a touch typist, but I type fairly fast. Another thing I notice is I begin to use more fingers than usual to type this paragraph. As I become more aware, my fingers are more dexterous. The movement of my hands becomes more smooth and fluid. Also, the usual pattern of which fingers I use for specific keys becomes more flexible and my repertoire expands so I am able to use different fingers which usually remain still.

I've also noticed I am able to use more fingers with my left hand than my right hand. Curious!

As you can see from my personal example, I was able to explore in the moment and didn't need to stop what I was doing. Even as I found the words to share the discoveries with you, I was able to continue typing.

You can do this every time you remember; with any task you are carrying out. Just become more aware, curious as to what you will notice.

There is no need to force any movement as you watch what you are doing. Allow any changes to happen and do your best not to judge them as better or worse.

By observing, just let whatever happens, naturally unfold by itself. Allow yourself to rest back in your experience and become the witness to every movement that unfolds before your eyes. Feel the sensations and see what else you notice.

If you notice tension in your body, just watch it without agenda or judgement and see if it releases or intensifies. To the best of your ability, have no need to change how you feel and instead just give more of your attention to what you are noticing and see what happens next.

Relaxing and softening of muscles happens by itself. If this isn't the case and an area of your body becomes more intense or painful, approach it with the question 'where can I do less?' Or notice if there is a feeling that wants to flow through your body which you are stopping or resisting?

If you can approach this exercise like it's a game or experiment, you will find you will discover more and the whole process will become light and easy.

Don't look for, or expect, a certain outcome. Treat the exercise as an ongoing exploration into becoming more in tune and familiar with yourself and the body you have.

Work with any disability or tension and allow the body to find its own way back into harmony with its natural state. Work with your environment and the objects you are in contact with at any given moment.

If it occurs to you to alter your seating or standing position, follow that intuition and see what happens. Sometimes I find it gets worse if I shift position, so I have to shift a few times and allow my body to take over and move itself into a more comfortable position, without my mind jumping in and taking over.

I've had to relearn how to walk again. It's not that I had forgotten, but I had so many habits I initiated as soon as I started walking, it has taken quite some time to get used to walking in a more natural way.

Like a baby learning to walk for the first time. It takes practice and can feel awkward and clumsy, until we relearn how to walk without slipping back into unnatural habits and postural deviations.

Thankfully my body knows how to move and all I need to do is be alert to how I am moving, and the body takes over and walks itself.

It really helps to be innocent and curious as much as you can.

Notice if dialogue pops up in your mind and refocus your attention back onto your body. As many times as you need to. Remember you are in training to become more present. It's like training at the gym. Keep applying the new focus onto your body and pay attention to what you see, hear, and feel.

If you get frustrated and/or pain intensifies to the point where it's intolerable, stop all movement and apply the instruction from the beginning of this exercise. You may need to hit an imaginary reset button before you go again! This may sound silly, but it works really well for me as a pattern interrupt. Plus, it usually makes me smile, so I lighten up a bit and my body follows suit.

Keep exploring whenever you remember and keep it simple and light-hearted, letting curiosity lead the way.

Chapter 44
Breath meditation

This chapter will provide you with a variety of different breath meditation exercises. Each exercise is beneficial in bringing movement and a greater supply of oxygen into the body, thereby increasing the body's ability to heal.

In addition to the physical benefit to the body, breath meditation calms and re-balances the entire system. When the body calms and relaxes, the mind follows, negative thinking reduces, and the mind will become quiet and still.

When the mind is still you can become much more aware of any place you are holding in and creating tension. As awareness increases you will find the tension dissolves by itself.

Breath exercises are therefore a good all-round tonic for the mind and body. With practice, your relationship with pain will begin to change and become more relaxed.

. . .

4×4 Breathing Technique

This technique is apparently used by the Navy Seals, because it allows them to remain calm and alert whilst on a mission.

In everyday life, living with chronic pain can feel like a mission in itself. This technique can calm and re-balance the mind and body almost immediately.

It is very basic and therefore simple and easy to remember, and practice. It's useful to practice with your eyes closed or open. You can pause and use it throughout the day with eyes open, or stop and sit/lie down for a deeper relaxation session.

Here is the instruction:

1. Breathe into the belly for the count of 4.

2. Hold for the count of 4.

3. Breathe out for the count of 4.

4. Hold for the count of 4.

5. Repeat 4 - 10 times.

Allow your breathing to be slow, smooth, and connected.

For a pause and reset session with your eyes open, repeating this exercise cycle 4 times is sufficient.

If you are anxious or in a great deal of pain, repeat the cycle until you feel the intensity calm down to a manageable level.

For greater impact, lie down or sit in a comfortable chair with your head supported. Carry out each cycle of 4 breaths very slowly and intend for your body to soften and relax more and more deeply with each cycle.

When you have completed approximately 10 cycles, rest for a moment and breathe gently into your belly. When you feel ready, very slowly, deliberately, and gently continue on with your day.

If you can do a more gentle or relaxing activity to begin with, e.g. reading a book, this will be more beneficial than going straight into a physical activity or stressful task.

. . .

Extension Breathing (4 - 8)

This breath exercise is very helpful if pain intensity is rapidly increasing, or in the sudden onset of a panic attack.

Slowly and evenly breathe into the belly following these instructions:

1. Breathe once, in for the count of 4 and out for the count of 4.

2. Then breathe in for the count of 4 and increase the out breath to the count of 5 for one breath.

3. Then breathe in for the count of 4 and increase the out breath to the count of 6 for one breath.

4. Then breathe in for the count of 4 and increase the out breath to the count of 7 for one breath.

5. For the last time, breathe in for the count of 4 and increase the out breath to the count of 8 for one breath.

6. Finish with a few slow, gentle, smooth, and easy breaths. This exercise is useful for acute pain, spasms and emotional overwhelm. Use eyes open or closed. After a short break, repeat steps 1-6 if you feel it would help you to stabilise your emotional state and/or level of pain.

. . .

The Pineal Gland Technique

Using this simple technique, which consists of abdominal breathing, visualization, and intonation (making a specific sound), may help you to sleep better and improve your overall state of health.

This technique will take about 15 minutes to do. It should be done each evening, preferably at bedtime, and can be performed lying down or sitting up.

1. For the first 5 minutes, focus on your breathing. Each in breath and out breath should be done through the nose and with the abdomen (not with the chest). Put your hand over your abdomen to feel it rise and fall. Spend the same amount of time on the in breath and out breath. Keep your breath connected, flowing, and smooth.

2. For the second 5 minutes, keep the breath smooth and on the inward breath through the nose, imagine you are making the pineal gland (in the centre of the skull) light up like an intensely bright light. It doesn't matter if you don't actually see a bright light. On the out breath, through the nose, imagine the pineal gland is sending the whole body what it needs to be healthy. If there is a specific area that needs healing, focus your attention on only that part of the body.

3. For the final 5 minutes, continue the same method for the in breath, and on the out breath make a sound "OM". At first this should be loud enough so you can hear it clearly, but with practice you can intone the sound quietly enough that someone sitting 15 feet away from you wouldn't be able to hear it. There are different sounds you can use, depending on what needs healing. If you don't have any specific problem, then use one of the sounds for your whole body, like OM.

1. Whole Body - OOM, OM, AMEN, YAH WAY
2. Thymus and Upper Chest - EHM (pronounced aim)
3. Thyroid - MER (pronounced mir)
4. Sinuses - MMM
5. Chest & Heart - AH, MA
6. Throat - EYE (pronounced I)
7. Brain - EEE
8. Prostrate, Genital Areas - UH
9. Lungs, Asthma – SSS
10. Back Pain - WOOO

Technique adapted from: Singh, Ranjie N. (1998) Self-Healing: Powerful Techniques. Health Psychology Associates Inc., London, ON, Canada. (pp. 51 & 52)

Chapter 45
Sound and vibration

Pain happens when we resist life and the body begins to hold tension. Holding tension is a forceful thing to do and it shuts down the natural functioning of the body, as I've already mentioned.

The antidote to tension is movement.

The more you can gently increase movement in the body, the more health and vitality you will experience.

This is why exercise is so beneficial for the body. So, what can you do if the level of pain, or restriction of mobility means you cannot exercise?

I came across sound as a means to bring movement into the body by accident. I was exploring Shamanic journeying and the course I attended used a drum to induce an altered state akin to hypnosis. I enjoyed the course and so I bought my own drum to experiment with at home.

One day whilst I was playing my drum (it was a 22-inch buffalo drum) my arms were aching due to the weight and so I changed position, with the drum now facing me. The minute I started drumming again in this position, the pain I was experiencing eased and a pleasant and soothing sensation flooded over me.

It was the vibration of the drum creating sound waves which passed through me. It felt so relaxing and enjoyable I continued drumming until my arms needed a rest. You cannot believe how much of a relief this was for me!

At the time I was in perpetual chronic pain which was almost unbearable, it was so intense and all encompassing. Pain medication did not work for me as I mentioned before.

So, to suddenly have the pain subside and a pleasurable sensation replace it, was a totally amazing and very welcome experience.

This discovery led me to explore the healing possibilities of sound vibration. Initially this exploration was for pain relief alone. Then I noticed, not only did the pain subside each time I directed the drum vibration onto my body, but the symptoms were beginning to reduce after a period of daily drumming sessions.

I experimented with singing bowls, rattles and any instrument which made a sound. All of them were useful if I could direct the sound waves at my body.

This wasn't always possible. And so, I explored what differences I could notice, even if the sound waves weren't directed at me. It was more subtle, but any music, or sound I could hear close-by had an impact on my body.

Sound, therefore, became more important to me. It appeared my new-found interest had opened up a world which presented me with new ways to explore and play with sound as a healing tool.

I discovered if I shook a rattle over my bed before sleeping, I would sleep better that night. If I shook a rattle over my stomach when I felt full and bloated, my stomach would gurgle and relax, and digestion would improve.

The list went on and on.

The drum was the most effective at bringing relief to the pain and encouraging my body to relax and feel better. Singing bowls were pleasant, soothing, and enjoyable to play. Rattles were great at relieving digestive issues and clearing stagnant energy in the home.

So, if you're interested, play and explore with a range of sounds and instruments to see what you discover for yourself.

Then there is music. Music has a more profound impact on our state of being than we often realise. We all know we enjoy listening to music and some songs can relax us, whilst others can energise us. But the effects of different types of music can be more impactful than just relaxing or uplifting our mood.

The impact increases when we pay full attention whilst we listen to music. If it's just playing in the background then we hear the song or instrumental track and enjoy it, but we don't fully engage with it.

To pay full attention means the music enters us and draws us into the world of the composer or artist. We feel the full sensory experience, and this can have a transformational effect on our mood, our body, and our thoughts. Thinking falls away and no longer directs the experience, so we can benefit from the full range of the musical experience.

Music and singing can be something you listen to or something you interact with. By that I mean singing and playing an instrument yourself.

Playing an instrument can be a cathartic and pleasurable experience if you surrender to the music and stop trying to make it sound nice.

This is surrender. Surrender is the path to peace.

If you already play an instrument, the next time you pick it up to play, treat it like an experiment. Surrender to the sound without any label of good or bad, better or worse, right or wrong.

Surrender and see what the music can show you.

This brings me to the instrument you were born with - your own voice.

We all have the capacity for a large range of sounds and yet we rarely use our own voice for anything more than speaking. Plus, when we are stressed and tense, we reduce the range of sound further. This can produce an almost monotone sound which is dull and lifeless or a strained higher pitch which can sound forceful.

One of the meanings of the name 'Meera' is 'The mystical singer'. When I received this name, I was of the opinion I could not sing. There was a reaction in me which was not comfortable with this meaning because it did not feel true.

However, shortly after receiving the name I confided in someone that I can't sing. They simply said, "how do you know"? This surprised me, but I had an answer. I knew because the last time I had tried to sing it had sounded awful and my children had told me to stop!

Although that was true, it was not the absolute truth. I began to recall a time when I was a young child and I used to sing all the time.

In receiving the name, it opened up a curiosity in me to see if I could sing again now. I quickly found I could in fact sing quite well, but not all the time. There was a hesitancy in me. I doubted that the next sound I made would be good. Then I remembered I had learned it wasn't always okay to make sounds. At certain times in my home when I was growing up, I was told I had to be quiet. I had essentially learned to silence my voice, in an environment where sound was sometimes unacceptable.

I had to unlearn that conditioning and start to explore my own voice. It was tentative at first and I'm still uncomfortable singing in front of other people at times. But more and more I am gaining in confidence and the sounds I make are more often pleasant, and the voice restriction and straining is reducing.

When I'm on my own I can explore my voice range without inhibition and the sounds are much purer and more melodic.

When there is someone else present, it can hinder my natural ability to just sing from the heart and enjoy the process.

It's a work in progress!

What is fascinating to me, and a source of further experimentation, is how much singing or just making any sound can resonate through my entire body and enliven every single part of me.

My son has also discovered that singing is useful in reducing the tension and pain he had been experiencing in his jaw. I have this same tension and so I am following his lead to see what happens when I sing or become playful. Allowing complete freedom to make any sound I like, without feeling stupid or self-conscious.

Humming is a helpful bridge to singing that feels more comfortable for me. And so often I will hum along to a tune if someone else is there. It's important not to force yourself if it doesn't feel safe or comfortable. I explore more fully when nobody else is around and this loosens me up to be more daring with other people present.

I also use 'sounding out' when something is painful and seems stuck. As I release all the stored tension and stresses from my nervous system, my body can become rigid and uncomfortable. It's rare that pain becomes intense these days, because I am so practiced at letting it move. But occasionally I get lost in the sensation, and either speaking about how I feel or sounding out can help it to shift and release.

This can look many different ways too. If my right hip is locked and pain increases and feels stuck, I will just 'say it how it is'. For example, I may say: "It really hurts" and then repeat if it stays stuck. This may ease the pain, or I may start moaning and allow the annoyance at the pain to express through me and resonate through my right hip. The movement through the physical body will often release the tension and the sensation in my hip will begin to ease off.

Annoyance can cause more tension if you resist the feeling though. In this case, I acknowledge the annoyance and let the emotion flow through me as best I can. The key is to let the emotion and stuck sensation move, even if only a little.

Again, play and explore and see what can help you. I would suggest you do it in private though. Even if you have family or friends who are open-minded and support you, it's never as liberating as when you are on your own, with no-one to comment on what you are doing or what results you are experiencing.

Never push yourself either. If the sensation is just stuck and the experiment begins to become forceful or frustrating, stop and try again later or another day.

You might find instead of sound you may feel like sighing, or coughing, or even laughing or crying. Surrender to the process and let whatever wants to happen, happen without judgement or constraint.

Again, gentleness and innocence are key to a more effective approach to changing your relationship with your body and painful sensations.

Chapter 46
Moving your awareness

Your awareness moves wherever you direct it. Awareness is the one thing we can control. It is also known as your attention.

You can always choose where to place your attention and what you want to be aware of.

This can work in our favour, or it can cause suffering.

Where we choose to place our attention, is where we live our life.

We have learnt to unconsciously place our attention on what we don't want, or don't like. We have done this, because we have learnt to believe we can change what we don't like or want, into something better.

The only problem with this approach is, what we put our attention on grows. The result of putting more of our attention on what we don't want is getting more of what we don't want and what we don't like!

This is a crazy and ineffective approach and one which causes much suffering and limitation.

We have developed very ingrained habits for where we place our attention. Very often we are running on an automatic unconscious program that directs our attention again and again, onto what we don't want. So, we need to counteract these habits and begin to direct our attention onto what we do want.

Everything is enlivened by giving it our attention. Choose wisely. If you notice you are focusing on what you don't want more of, simply choose again.

You can become much more aware if you choose each time you notice you are focusing on what you don't want.

An uncomfortable feeling is a clear sign that you are focusing on what you don't want. For example, it could be something unpleasant which happened in the past. Even if it was only minutes ago.

The moment you notice what you are doing, stop. Stop and take a breath. Then divert your focus onto something pleasant, something uplifting, something you actually do want. Preferably something that is here and now, and relevant to this moment.

You cannot change the past, but you can leave it behind and focus on pastures new.

In order to prevent the same dialogue, the same situations and conversations from repeating again and again, you need to use a new approach.

Stop. Pause. And change your focus. If you have to choose a thousand times a day, keep making the choice.

Three for One

To redress the balance, choose 'three things' which are pleasant, for every time you notice your focus is on 'one thing' that is not pleasant.

If you are criticising something or someone, think of three things you can appreciate about the situation, event or person and notice if that changes how you feel.

Then drop it and go about your day anew, with a fresh perspective.

Noticing the Moment exercise

This little exercise is great for bringing us gently from the past or future into this moment. Do each part slowly and gently; pause to explore before moving onto the next step.

1. Begin by paying attention to the soles of your feet. Notice what they are in contact with, what that feels like and just observe.

2. Then shift your attention to the palms of your hands. What does that feel like? Just notice and pay gentle attention.

3. Now move your attention to the tip of your nose and notice the air moving in and out of your nose. Is it warm, cool? What is the sensation like? Just notice.

4. Then draw your attention into your belly and watch. Observe the sensations and be gently attentive to them.

5. Next, become aware of the space around your body.

6. Slowly expand your awareness to the space around you. Become aware of all the air in the room that you are in.

7. Expand your awareness further, to incorporate the whole house, or building you are in right now.

8. Then expand it even more to the space around your house or building.

9. Just notice that this moment is happening.

10. Gently rest there for a few moments and then slowly continue on with your day.

Now you have a couple of different ways to activate new habits which will help you to become more focused and one-pointed on that which you do want. That which you want more of. The exercises will help you to become present to this moment, so you become aware of all the opportunities and possibilities that are available to you.

When you are present you will see more and notice more. The blinkers of the limited thinking patterns are removed, and you can see and hear, without the filters of your mind limiting your experience.

Chapter 47
Loving the skin you're in

We are very good at judging our bodies. It's too fat, too thin, the wrong colour, the wrong shape and so the list goes on.

This judgement comes from a core belief that we are not good enough, or not loveable.

The belief is false and serves no purpose. One of the best ways to overcome this belief is to stop listening to the whispering voice that is telling you what is wrong with your body.

The first step in my experience is to acknowledge the way your body is right now.

It's not good or bad, it just is.

Your body may need a little help to be fit and healthy, but it is not bad or wrong the way it is right now. That's an important step to take, to become neutral and just acknowledge what is. To acknowledge prevents denial, reduces self-criticism, and brings you into the present moment.

The present moment is the place where you can gain clarity on what does or doesn't need to be done. This clarity will guide you on a course of action, and you will be able to see many more options available to you than the thinking mind has access to.

In this clear state, you will perceive your body differently. The judgement is no longer present and so the mind's perceived blemishes may be seen as beautiful instead of ugly. Anything that needs to be done for your body to remain healthy will become apparent.

Acknowledgement is the pathway to acceptance, appreciation, and gratitude.

When we get good at simply acknowledging our body, we will naturally become more accepting of it. With the acceptance comes an appreciation of what our body does for us every day. You begin to see the complexity and intelligence of your body, and this appreciation turns into a deep sense of gratitude.

Then and only then, can we love the skin we're in.

Acceptance is not as difficult or complicated as we sometimes make it out to be.

We don't need to accept a poor state of health as our lot in life. That is not what I mean. That is apathy.

What I mean, is to accept what is. To simply recognise that what is happening, is happening and stop fighting against the current state of your body.

Why would we do that? Because fighting what is, is futile and causes suffering.

When we lay down our sword and accept the state our body is in right now, our body can relax and heal. Our body can work more efficiently and suffering ends.

When suffering ceases, we become full of appreciation for our body. Our eyes are opened to all the benefits and beauty our body has to offer.

If we remain in this state of appreciation, we naturally develop a greater and deeper sense of gratitude for our body.

As we soften and relax into a state of gratitude, our body receives a deep and restorative rest and we learn to love the body we have.

When we love our body, we are much more considerate towards it. Not just as a concept or hollow words, but as a direct experience of unconditional love. We can then treat it with the respect it deserves and become much more gentle in our approach, looking after its needs. We can actually be kind to our body and this kindness is so profoundly nurturing and beneficial.

Think of your body as a sacred temple and look after it. If you do that, your body temple will be in a better state of repair and it will look better and work so much more efficiently and easily.

All this begins with the first easy step of acknowledgment.

Take one baby step at a time and if you fall down, just like a toddler learning to walk, pick yourself up and go again.

Gentleness and persistence, along with respect and kindness will produce results. Thus allowing ourselves to be exactly as we are, without judgement. We can grow fast when we are nurtured and well-cared for.

There is a simple visualisation technique that is really beneficial and useful for changing our relationship with ourselves and others. It's called 'the pink light technique'. It is very gentle and yet powerful at transforming the way we perceive ourselves and the world around us.

This technique is best used innocently with no agenda or expectation of any particular result. The greatest results happen when we stop trying to make something change and innocently explore what happens when we simply use the technique daily for a while.

I would recommend you practice this technique for at least 21 days. This is the period of time it takes to change a habit and create a new one. If you can commit to practicing this technique for 6 weeks, you will likely notice even greater, more sustainable results. But be open to what the results may be, and brush aside any assessment of results until you have practiced it for more than 21 days.

. . .

The Pink Light Technique

The following technique is a powerful healing tool to be used once daily. This technique is ancient in origin and has been used throughout the millennia to heal relationships. It has never been known to fail. This technique has been effectively used to heal all pain and suffering between the user and the subject. Use the technique in innocence and without conditions. It is miraculous!

1. Get yourself in a loving space. Remember a time when you felt loved.

2. In your mind's eye, picture Pink Loving Light radiating from your heart, encompassing you in a Pink Sphere.

3. Stay within your Pink Light Sphere… remember a most loving memory of yourself (this could be recent or from your childhood) and project this aspect of you outside of the Pink Light Sphere. Cover this projection of yourself with the Pink Loving Light (radiating from your heart).

4. Then, starting with your immediate family - mother, father, siblings, partner, children - individually imagine them in front of you, outside the Pink Light Sphere. When possible, have the image of them in a loving memory. In your mind's eye, picture yourself covering each of them with the Pink Light (as if you were icing a cake). Cover them, and then let them go and move on to the next person. (If you cannot remember this person in a loving memory, just picture them in front of you. If you cannot do this, then bring them in, standing at a distance and/or facing away from you).

5. Next, bring in anyone with whom you still have an emotional charge or discomfort. (Follow the instructions above).

6. Allow for anyone else to show up (whoever needs to be brought into your awareness is ok, whether you know them or not), cover them with the Pink Loving Light and let them go as well.

Note: In the beginning, this process should take no more than ten minutes a day, eventually getting down to five minutes. If you can't visualize the Pink Light, that is fine, the intent is what is important.

Once someone is done, assume they are finished for the day. You will get a sense when someone is complete and no longer requires a treatment. Some people will not show up for a while; others that you didn't expect to see will suddenly appear to receive the Pink Light.

This technique has had great success for those who have been raped, molested or abused. Runaway children have been known to reconnect with their family within weeks of this technique being implemented. Although most people using this technique find it easy to do, some – principally cancer patients – have great difficulty doing Step 3.

NB: Remember to do yourself every time you use the technique.

Chapter 48
Keep making the choice

Just knowing you have a choice is the first step to changing your relationship with pain. But it's not enough to understand this choice theoretically. Dry facts are useful to know and some people have found the pain goes away, just in understanding the process. However, to be able to make a sustainable change, it is necessary to combine the theory with direct experience.

In essence, by combining theory and experience, we make the unconscious conscious. For example, if you think of the unconscious as a dark room and consciousness as the light, you cannot switch the light on by understanding the process. You actually need to flip the switch to turn on the light. In order to be able to see and work in the room, you will need to keep the light turned on.

It's the same with consciousness. To change your relationship with pain, you need to be conscious of all the patterns of thought and habitual responses which are keeping pain in play. Only when you are conscious, can you change what is causing or contributing towards the pain.

Continual investigation is required to uncover all these patterns, which can only be revealed when the light is on, when we are consciously aware of them.

Using this same analogy, what can happen and feel disturbing or stop the process, can be the light going off when we are in the room investigating. This can feel disturbing and will limit our investigation.

I have often tried to continue my exploration in the dark. It is very uncomfortable and actually quite fruitless and ineffective. We need the light on to see what is <u>actually</u> real and what is <u>actually</u> occurring. We can then make clear and rational decisions or carry out the necessary steps to reduce painful symptoms.

This brings me to talk about a typical approach of soothing symptoms. Most of us are used to soothing symptoms, as if it's the only choice we have to reduce or stop pain. Whilst it's okay to soothe symptoms of course, it can often be counterproductive.

This is because in soothing the symptoms, you are paying attention to them, which keeps the symptoms at the forefront of your awareness, and they remain in place. You can reduce symptoms and halt them for a period of time. But unless you identify and remove the root cause, they will always come back, or manifest as a different symptom. By soothing the symptoms, you could be missing the root cause.

I still use methods to soothe symptoms and in some cases it is necessary. For example, in order to breathe and have enough oxygen in my system to operate, I need to use an inhaler to control the symptoms.

Yet the most important thing for me, is to uncover and change the underlying pattern causing the symptoms. I am learning there are times it is best not to soothe or try to reduce or eliminate the symptoms.

This is because it keeps them in play and has no impact on them in the long run. So, I sit with the discomfort and (through my Ascension practice) I have learnt to observe without agenda and the symptoms often dissolve.

I see it as a retraining process. It's like I turn on the light, and darkness (pain) vanishes without a trace. Then through habit the light switches off and the symptoms / pain returns.

All I have to do is switch the light back on and all is well. The only hurdle to this very simple process is, I can't always find the light switch to be able to turn it back on.

It is a moment by moment choice. As we proceed in continually making the choice, the choice will get easier to make.

At one point, I recognised if I have zero interest in movement, my ability to be alert to the choice is much more obvious and easier to implement.

By 'zero interest in movement' I mean I no longer make the symptoms the focus. Symptoms are the content; they are movement to the context of stillness. It is a subtle shift to make, but to cultivate and maintain a focus of attention on stillness means the movement can be fluid and nurturing, rather than restricted and dysfunctional.

The Ascension techniques automatically strengthen the ability to focus on the still part of the experience. I make the choice, every time I recognise, I'm focused on the content of symptoms and trying to control the movement.

I'm grateful I have the choice and know how to make it! As I have consistently made this choice, my relationship with symptoms and pain has changed dramatically for the better. Plus, my body now works much more effectively, and I maintain a greater level of overall health and well-being.

When pain or symptoms appear, I simply return my attention to stillness. In doing this, some symptoms simply disappear, others are put back into context; suffering ends and I am able to function as well as experience peace.

Maintaining a focus on stillness is like building a house on rock. Whereas trying to change or control symptoms and pain, is like living in a house built on sand.

When a house is built on sand, as you can imagine, it shifts and moves continually when the weather becomes stormy. If a house is built on rock it can withstand any amount of adverse weather conditions and remain stable and secure.

If you remain focused and intent on changing your symptoms, you will get pulled around or even sucked into the experience and become submerged in pain and suffering. For me it is obvious our past habits will muddy the waters and cloud the mind, so we cannot see what step to take, or not to take.

I recommend you investigate for yourself. Keep exploring the suggestions, concepts, and exercises in this book. Ultimately it is the experience that has the greatest impact, not what you understand, so the exercises are the most important part.

Prioritise your peace and learn how to still the mind. Then you will have an increased chance of changing your relationship with pain, and suffering will end.

The Ascension techniques are the tools which have given me the continual and automatic return to peace. These tools work! They work like magic every single time I use them. With no effort they take you directly to an experience of stillness, which is where you can experience peace.

My life has become all about living without an explanation, without apology, without a need to do something to be acceptable to other people. I am free to be myself and my body is grateful for this. The freedom of being myself takes the pressure off my body.

I've discovered it's not about feeling better, it's about not arguing with how you do feel. Acceptance of 'what is' means you drop the fight and are then able to see more clearly what course of action is suitable.

Reducing intensity levels requires agreeing with how you feel. Acknowledge what you notice and allow movement.

In short, go with the flow of life, in your body and in your interaction with the world around you.

An experience of the still, silent presence is the most important step you will ever take in the journey to become pain free. However, with chronic pain, serious health conditions, emotional overwhelm and mental trauma, it is important that you seek guidance from a medical doctor.

With the appropriate help and support to take care of your mental and physical state, explore how to become fully present with the pain.

Peace is available and possible for every single person. It is possible to change your relationship with pain, it is possible to choose peace over pain.

Make the choice for peace whenever you remember.

Don't think about it … Just do it!

"Ascension is the most useful peace-building tool, because it stops the cycle of reaction."

- Sri Ishaya -

Appendix

Resources

Ascension: To find out more about the Ascension techniques and the teaching of The Bright Path Ishayas please visit the website: www.thebrightpath.com

Reviews: If you have found the contents of this book helpful, please leave a review on Amazon to help others find this book and discover the possibility of choice. Gratitude to all who choose to leave a positive review!

Videos and Webinars: Recordings of previous webinars are available on a variety of health issues and approaches to changing your relationship with pain. Go to the YouTube channel 'Meera Ishaya'. Please subscribe, like and share with friends, colleagues and family who may also benefit from watching these videos.

Share: Please let others know about this book or buy them a copy!

Podcasts/Seminars/YouTube/Television: I am open to appearing on any platform to talk about my relationship with pain and what people can do to discover peace.

If you would like me to come and give a talk, workshop or interview please email me at: info@boundless-meditation.co.uk

Website: For more information go to: www.boundless-meditation.co.uk

Appendix

Suicide Watch

The first chapter in this book describes a very difficult time in my life. It's not something I share lightly. But it was the turning point in my life, and it felt important to share it with you.

I hope if you have any thoughts about suicide, you find a way to get the help you need. The help each person actually needs is individual to their own requirements.

For me I couldn't take any more physical pain. But as I've learnt over the years since that moment, pain can be mental torment or emotional overload just as much as physical pain.

There is always an answer to your personal trauma. There is always help. Always someone who cares.

Each and every person is important and valuable in this world. Humanity needs everyone to make the inner change towards peace, love, and kindness. We need everyone to find a way to step through the pain and discomfort and learn to simply be ourselves.

We all have skills and talents which are useful to others. Useful to bring humanity together to work as one.

I overcame the desire to end my life and now I love being alive. It was not always easy though.

I want to share a story with you about a good friend of mine, Amanda. I had spontaneously phoned her one day and we were having the usual friendly and frank conversation.

I then told her about an article I had just read, which had profoundly touched me. It was about people who had jumped off the Golden Gate bridge to end their life. A small percentage of people survive the jump, which I found incredible.

What really intrigued me though, was the fact that every single one of the people who survived the jump, said they changed their mind the minute they let go of the railings and fell.

What got me thinking and was the question I posed to my friend, was - Did they survive because they changed their mind and realised they wanted to live? Or did everyone change their mind, but only the lucky few survived to tell the tale?

We finished our conversation and arranged to meet the next week for coffee. I thought nothing more of it and had no idea what Amanda would share with me when we met up the following week.

Half-way through our conversation, Amanda leaned in and shared a revelation that was a shock to me.

The day I had called her and shared my thoughts about the Golden Gate bridge survivors, she had planned to end her life. I knew she had previously had these thoughts, but I did not know she had got to that place again.

She told me the Golden Gate bridge story I shared with her, helped her to change her mind. Because of this and another friend who took her for a walk that day, she chose to live.

I was shocked to say the least. Not so much that she was serious about ending her life, but because I had no idea her state of mind was so low again.

Whether it was my intuition, or pure chance, I am very grateful that I said what I did and somehow reached her in such a profound way. At the time, I didn't realise how timely my phone call conversation was.

The world is full of traumatised people who need help, love and support. Reach out to friends and family. Make sure they feel loved and know how important they are to you.

And if you feel like ending your life, please please please, reach out and ask for help.

You may be in a world of torment and pain, physically, mentally and/or emotionally. But there is a way out of the pain and suffering. There is an answer for you. There is a solution: a way to feel worthwhile, happy, and loved.

We are not meant to go through this life alone. We are most effective when we join together and work as a team. Whether that is two people or a whole bunch, connecting and sharing.

I was told once, many years ago, there are 3 components to happiness:

1. Community

2. Service

3. Growth

Since that time, I have discovered this is true, over and over again. We need to find as many ways as possible to connect, share ideas, share love, and feel part of a community.

Having spent a large part of my life feeling lost, alone, left out, I can honestly say having found my 'tribe' within the Ishaya community has been a life saver.

I finally feel at home. At home in my own skin and in a community of people who are kind, loving but also weird and wonderful too. All willing to be themselves, no matter what others say. And that is very cool.

It is also a huge relief.

Service is also something that provides so much fulfilment in my personal life. When you are in your own head, struggling and battling with yourself, with others and even life in general, stopping and doing something for someone else has the knock-on effect of stopping the inner destructive dialogue.

You can feel useful, by giving service. You will always receive something in return, and you find happiness in places you would never have thought to look.

Then there is growth. We are either growing, or dying, in each and every moment. So choose to grow. Look for places to stretch yourself, to learn something new, to go beyond your current skill set and explore what else is available.

Inner growth is the most valuable way to grow in my eyes. It is more sustainable and beneficial to explore who we really are, beyond the thoughts, emotions, and body sensations.

To 'know thyself' changes your experience of life in the most surprising, delightful and enjoyable way.

We are not meant to go it alone, so I highly recommend you find 'your tribe'. Find ways to serve in your community and find ways to continually grow.

If you don't know how, ask for help. Or just do one small thing, one small step and let the universe lead you to the next chapter of your life.

Ascension is what made the biggest difference for me and could also be your best chance to live a happy and fulfilling life. Go and check it out...

Printed in Great Britain
by Amazon

66897937R00149